Praise for *First You Write a Sentence*

"Thoughtful reflections on how to write well . . . Moran is a thoroughly sane, thoughtful commentator."
—*The Guardian* (Book of the Week)

"Joe Moran is a wonderfully sharp writer, calm, precise, and quietly comical. . . . Moran's own sentences are perfect advertisements for the aims they espouse. . . . He writes with a playful clarity that makes *First You Write a Sentence* a joy to read."
—*The Mail on Sunday* (UK)

"It takes chutzpah to write a book about writing sentences. Between every full stop lies the potential to fail by your own standards, as countless style guide writers have done before. But Joe Moran has a perfect ear for English. *First You Write a Sentence* is an edifying joy."
—Lynne Murphy, author of *The Prodigal Tongue: The Love-Hate Relationship Between American and British English*

"Thoughtful, engaging, and lively exposé of the quirks and beauties of the full sentence . . . It's a style guide by stealth: when you've read it, you realize you've changed your attitude to writing (and reading)."
—John Simpson, former chief editor of the *Oxford English Dictionary* and author of *The Word Detective*

"What a lovely thing this is: a book that delights in the sheer textural joy of good sentences. Joe Moran has written a book about writing that is itself a collection of sentences to inspire, divert, and console. Any writer should read it, if only to be reminded how crazily hard it is to write words 'in such a way that they can be decip'
—Bee Wilso〔 〕 *First Bite*

PENGUIN BOOKS

FIRST YOU WRITE A SENTENCE

Joe Moran is a professor of English and Cultural History at Liverpool John Moores University.

First You Write a Sentence.

The Elements of Reading, Writing . . . and Life.

JOE MORAN

PENGUIN BOOKS

PENGUIN BOOKS
An imprint of Penguin Random House LLC
penguinrandomhouse.com

First published in Great Britain by Viking,
an imprint of Penguin Random House UK 2018
Published in Penguin Books (USA) 2019

Permission to quote the work of Ian Hamilton Finlay courtesy of
the Estate of Ian Hamilton Finlay; permission to quote the work of Robert
Montgomery courtesy of Robert Montgomery; permission to quote the
work of Martin Firrell courtesy of Martin Firrell (www.martinfirrell.com)

LIBRARY OF CONGRESS CATALOGING-IN-PUBLICATION DATA
Names: Moran, Joe, 1970- author.
Title: First you write a sentence : the elements of reading,
writing...and life / Joe Moran.
Description: [New York] : Penguin Books, 2019. | "First published in Great Britain
by Viking, an imprint of Penguin Random House UK, 2018"—Title page verso. |
Includes bibliographical references and index. |
Identifiers: LCCN 2018058377 (print) | LCCN 2019007226 (ebook) |
ISBN 9780525506157 (ebook) | ISBN 9780143134343 (trade pbk.)
Subjects: LCSH: English language—Sentences. | Creative writing. |
Creative writing—Social aspects.
Classification: LCC PE1441 (ebook) | LCC PE1441 .M665 2019 (print) |
DDC 808/.042—dc23
LC record available at https://lccn.loc.gov/2018058377

Printed in the United States of America
1   3   5   7   9   10   8   6   4   2

Set in Dante MT Std

Contents

For first you write a sentence,
  And then you chop it small;
Then mix the bits, and sort them out
  Just as they chance to fall:
The order of the phrases makes
  No difference at all.

Lewis Carroll, "Poeta Fit, Non Nascitur" ("A Poet is Made, Not Born"), in *Phantasmagoria and Other Poems* (1869)

Lytton Strachey said to me: first I write one sentence: then I write another. That's how I write. And so I go on. But I have a feeling writing ought to be like running through a field.

Max Beerbohm, quoted in Virginia Woolf's diary, 1 November 1938

A Pedant's Apology

Or why I wrote this book

First I write a sentence. I get a tickle of an idea for how the words might come together, like an angler feeling a tug on the rod's line. Then I sound out the sentence in my head. Then I tap it on my keyboard, trying to recall its shape. Then I look at it and say it aloud, to see if it sings. Then I tweak, rejig, shave off a syllable, swap a word for a phrase or a phrase for a word. Then I sit it next to other sentences to see how it behaves in company. And then I delete it all and start again.

If there were a pie chart that divided up my time on earth, the colored slice that covers writing sentences would be the biggest, apart from the one that covers the thing everyone does: sleeping. I don't count how much writing I have done each day, but if I did I wouldn't count words, I'd count sentences. Sentences are my core output, the little widgets I make in my workshop of words. It helps to think of it like this, as just cranking out a daily quota of sentences, instead of being a *writer*, which feels like a claim that will need to be stamped and approved. I write maybe three and a half thousand sentences a year. Is this too many, or not enough, or about right? I have no idea. I write one sentence, then another, and repeat until done. I don't know when *done* is.

Some writers claim to have sentences in their heads hollering to get out. Flaubert wrote that he was "itching" with them. These writers just seem to have a knack for putting words into right-seeming order, as if it were a skill as randomly allotted as being able to wiggle one's ears. Not me. But I can spot a good tune when

I hear it. I know what a good sentence looks and sounds like, so that when I come across one in my own writing I have the good sense not to delete it but to try and replicate it. Having only minor gifts has its compensations. It has forced me to think hard about how words join up and why some sentences work better than others. A nightingale has no idea why such a bewitching noise emerges from its throat; a human nightingale impersonator must parse every note.

I may give more time to them than most people do, but we are all of us, of school age and older, in the sentences game. Sentences are our writing commons, the shared ground where every writer walks. A poet works with them, but so does the unsung author who came up with *Items trapped in doors cause delays* or *Store in a cool, dry place*. Every kind of writer writes in sentences. Even the most clueless or careless strew their writing with capital letters and full stops, in the hope that they will turn what lies between them into this universal currency. By learning to make sentences, we learn not just about writing but about everything. The sentence is where we make the briefest of senses out of this mad, beautiful, befuddling mess: life.

•

In 1940 a soon-to-retire Cambridge math don called G. H. Hardy published a defense of his life's work. His field was the purest form of mathematics, number theory, and his book was meant to be a mea culpa for spending his life on something of no practical use that few people would ever understand. In fact, although he called it *A Mathematician's Apology*, it was not very apologetic.

Hardy declared that math had given him his life's "one great permanent happiness," and that, when the world was immolating itself in war, it offered a consolingly parallel universe of spare, numbered beauty. Applied math, the kind that could compute the dimensions of the Forth Bridge or the reach of a radio transmitter, he decried as "trivial." Real math, he thought, bypassed the world in pursuit of pure abstraction. It was useful only rarely and never on purpose. Like Einstein, Hardy felt above all that equations should be beautiful. "A mathematician, like a painter or a poet," he wrote, "is a maker of patterns."

A mathematical equation and a written sentence have much in common. Both rely on symmetry and balance, often asserting a connection between the seemingly different. Both explain reality in as elegantly concise a form as they can. Both reduce randomness to inevitability, their equal signs or clauses falling into place with a rightness that renders the inchoate and incoherent suddenly clear. Both tell us something about the world outside themselves—but both also swim in their own kind of beauty.

Pure mathematicians, like Hardy, have long debated whether advances in their field are invented or discovered. Is an elegant equation a piece of human handiwork, or the unearthing of an eternal reality that was there before some fortunate human chanced upon it? The same question might be asked of an elegant sentence, which seems to sit somewhere in this Tom Tiddler's ground between invention and discovery. Like an elegant equation, it has floated free of its maker and feels inevitable. It came out of a single mind but now belongs to the world.

Fixating on how a sentence looks and sounds, finding the right fit between the thought you want to express and the form it fits inside, can seem as removed from the real world as G. H. Hardy's mathematics. More so, perhaps, because, as Hardy wrote, human languages die but numbers live forever. To care about sentences as Hardy did about math, you must feel about them the way that he felt about numbers. In other words, you must know that, even as they try to explain and account for the world, nothing lies behind them but their own artifice.

•

Hardy's book has been an unlikely inspiration for mine. For this is a book of sentences written in praise of writing sentences. I want it not to school but to hearten, embolden and galvanize the reader—who is almost always, in some way, a writer. I hope it will say something useful about how to write a sentence and put it alongside other sentences. But really it is about why it is worth taking pains over a sentence, in a world where everyone seems to be speaking at once and finishing each other's sentences for them.

A lesson works best when it doesn't feel like one, when it feels instead like an attempt to repay the favor that was once done to the teacher—in my case, by the writers of other sentences that have instructed me in and delighted me into writing my own. So this book is not a style guide, if that means a series of prescriptions and proscriptions. But perhaps it is a style guide by stealth: one that tries to show what it wants to teach, or to show instead of teaching.

I was going to call it *A Pedant's Apology*—a mea culpa for spending my life worrying about something as small and minor-seeming as the sentence. But I am not sure I quite cut it as a pedant. Like most of my generation, my knowledge of grammar is a patchwork, sewn over many years and with thousands of holes in it.

I am still baffled by those sentence diagrams with the subject on the left and the verb on the right of a horizontal line, and modifiers veering off like motorway slip roads. However hard I try, I cannot link them in my head to actual sentences, the ones that are just a deceptively simple line of words. One of my sixth-form teachers told us that sentence diagrams were as vital to the study of sentences as skeletons were to a medical student studying anatomy. If she was right, then I will never be a doctor of writing. I scrabble my way through my own sentences on hunches and happenstance.

But then I remind myself that the English sentence belongs to everyone, not just those who like to police other people's use of it. I dislike writing advice that worries only about the sameness of surface features and that minds more about meticulousness than music. The literal meaning of *meticulous* is "being careful out of fear." Fear feels like the wrong feeling with which to start making sentences. For me it is not the veneration of rules but care for word choice and order that counts. If you get those right then all the rest of it, from dangling modifiers to Oxford commas, will solve itself or cease to matter.

And yet they do say that poets are pedants in disguise (or is it the other way round?). Even poets with a shaky grip on grammar care about where a comma falls or a full stop comes to rest. They know that it adds not just to the meaning of a line but to its music. For those of us who cannot do number theory, the sentence might be as near as we ever get to orchestrating beauty. A modest beauty, perhaps, which is all a sentence can aim at, but beauty all the same—one that turns the everyday words everyone uses into hard little jewels that glint and gleam together. If this is pedantry, then I plead guilty.

•

No one can agree on what a sentence is. The safest definition is typographic. A sentence starts with a capital letter and ends with a full stop—except that some start with quote marks, and some end with question or exclamation marks, so that doesn't quite work. Let's try again. A sentence is the largest domain over which the rules of grammar have dominion. Thus it stands grammatically apart from the sentences around it. Except when it is a fragment that hangs over from the last sentence as an afterthought. Or that briefly sets a scene, like every sentence of the shipping forecast. *Occasional gales. Fog patches. Mainly moderate.*

A sentence is a small, sealed vessel for holding meaning. It delivers some news—an assertion, command or question—about the world. Every sentence needs a subject, which is a noun or noun phrase, and a predicate, which is just the bit of the sentence that isn't the subject and that must have a main verb. The subject is usually (but not always) what the sentence is about and the predicate is usually (but not always) what happens to the subject or what it is. *This* [subject] *is a sentence* [predicate]. A sentence must have a subject and a main verb, except when it leaves out one or both of them because their presence is implied. OK?

A sentence can be a single word, or it can stretch into infinity, because more words can be piled on to a main clause for ever. The Czech writer Bohumil Hrabal wrote a whole novel (*Dancing Lessons for the Advanced in Age*) containing just one sentence. But he said that his comic sensibility was shaped by a short one he once read on a dry cleaner's receipt: *Some stains can be removed only by the destruction of the material itself.* Marcel Proust, who in *The Captive* wrote a 447-word sentence about a sofa, said that he wanted to "weave these long silks as I spin them" and to "encircle the truth with a single—even if long and sinuous—stroke." For Proust, a sentence traced an unbroken line of thought. Cutting it in two broke the line. Depending on its line of thought, a sentence can be a tiny shard of sense or a Proustian demi-world, brought to life and lit up with words.

For Henry David Thoreau, the sentence was the harvest gleaned in a writer's brain. "The fruit a thinker bears is *sentences*," he wrote in his journal. For Marianne Moore, the sentence exerted a pull on her "as the pull of a fabric is governed by gravity." For James Baldwin, the one true goal was "to write a sentence as clean as a bone." For John Cheever, "every sentence is an innovation," something never thought, never mind said, in quite that way before. For Annie Dillard, the sentence is a writer's true medium, and a writer with no feel for the sentence is not a writer, because that would be like being a painter who could not bear the smell of paint. For Gary Lutz, the sentence is our "one true theater of endeavor." For Maggie Nelson, the sentence is something to "labor grimly on ... wondering all the while if prose is but the gravestone marking the forsaking of wildness." For John Banville, the sentence is "this essential piece of our humanness ... our greatest invention."

Skilled writers write in sentences—not because sentences are what we all write in (although they are), but because they write small. They see the sentence as the *ur*-unit, the granular element that must be got right or nothing will be right. Their books, however long they become, are gatherings of sentences. Scientists at the Institute of Nuclear Physics in Kraków analyzed more than a hundred classic works by authors such as Dickens, Joyce and Beckett, and found that the sentences behaved like a mathematical multifractal: a structure whose smallest part resembles its whole. The best writing is self-consistent. It sounds as if it comes from the same breathing body standing in the same place, rather as wine from a certain *terroir* is said to have, from its climate and soil, a taste irreplicable anywhere else. What special *terroir* makes a piece of writing irreplicable? Its sentences.

Dedicated birdwatchers can identify a bird even when they do not have time to note its distinguishing marks of plumage and song. A skilled birder can tell you the breed from its general impression, size and shape, even if it is just a blur flying past in the dusk. A writer's voice is like that, too, perhaps. A skilled reader can spot it from a single sentence flashing by.

•

A sentence is more than its meaning. It is a line of words where logic and lyric meet—a piece of both sense and sound, even if that sound is heard only in the head. Things often thought to be peculiar to poetry—meter, rhythm, music—are there in prose as well, or should be. When John Betjeman began a BBC radio talk with the sentence "We came to Looe by unimportant lanes," he must have known it sounded better than "We drove to Looe via the minor roads." His version is ten syllables with the stress on each second syllable: a perfect iambic pentameter.

Some writers map their sentences metrically, marking the stressed and unstressed syllables with scansion marks as if notating a musical score. Some even work out the stresses before they fill in the words. The rest of us just have a foggy sense that a sentence needs an extra beat. But we still know that a sentence is not just what it says but how it says it. Robert Frost called this its "sound of sense," the emotional truth you could grasp even if you heard the sentence spoken by a muffled voice in another room. Here, he felt, beneath the mere grammatical obedience, were "the brute tones of our human throat that may once have been all our meaning."

Rookie sentence writers are often too busy worrying about the something they are trying to say to worry enough about how that something looks and sounds. They look straight past the words into the meaning that they have strong-armed into them. They fasten on content and forget about form—forgetting that content and form are the same thing, that what a sentence says *is* how it says it, and vice versa.

Rhythm is so basic to language that it does not need to be taught. You can correct a child's syntax and pronunciation, but if they have no feel for the rhythms of speech, they will not sound human. The rhythm of English stresses certain syllables within each word and certain words within each sentence. It makes us linger on nouns, adjectives and verbs and skip lightly over pronouns, conjunctions and prepositions. Hence we will never love the automated sentences of satnavs and public address systems, with their random rise and fall.

Rhythm is the song of life. The syllabic stress patterns of speech sync up with the heartbeat we hear in the womb, the pulses of air in the lungs, the strides of walking and running. Beating a rhythm is our first music, the joyous reflex that makes us tap feet, drum fingers and clap hands. To the young man carrying a pair of battered drumsticks everywhere in his back pocket, or the musicians of remote tribes who commandeer a river as a drum kit, their hands working up pops and thuds on the water as beatboxers do with their voices, the rhythmic urge must be obeyed. The music critic Ian Penman, writing about Grace Jones, called rhythm "song's manacle and its demonic charge ... the original breath ... the whisper of unremitting demand."

Rhythm holds meaning. Great orators make the rhythm of the words resound in our brains and bones before we work out what they have said. The rhythm wins us over—is "proved upon our pulses," as Keats put it—and then the sense catches up. I like to hear sentences read aloud, in public readings in echoey halls, or audiobooks coming through my earphones as I pace the streets, or radio essays I listen to under the duvet in the dark, the speaker's timbre sending me to sleep like a cradle song.

I haunt the corridors of my university building, speaking sentences under my breath. Those who know me know to ignore me. Sometimes I walk round the block doing the same thing, and passing strangers are surely less forgiving. Talk to yourself at work and you are just sounding out your thoughts; talk to yourself in the street and others look away and give you plenty of pavement. But it all helps, I tell myself, to lock the rhythms of writing into the skull. "Read good books, have good sentences in your ears," the poet Jane Kenyon advised—and a true and useful sentence can survive even a comma splice like that.

•

Bad grammar is usually a sign of something deeper amiss with the rhythm. More can go awry in a sentence than syntactical exactitude. Worse than the words being wrongly arranged is putting them in an order that neither moves nor sings. The sentence just limps and wheezes along to its sad end with a tuneless clank. When the writer has a tin ear for the sound of a sentence then the reader knows, just as when she hears flat or pitchy singing, that something is wrong, even if she can't quite say why.

I can let a book fall open and tell, just from reading a few sentences, if I will like it. However compelling the subject of a book might be, I find it hard to carry on reading if its sentences are boring. I should be more forgiving, since I have written my share of boring sentences. I am not. Neither are you, even if you don't know it yet. You think you are looking past this sentence into what it is saying—about life, love, the existence of angels, the design of the injection-molded polypropylene stacking chair, whatever it is—but no. You think you care what this book is about, but really you care how it sounds. You are reading it for its sentences.

I read cookery books by my favorite food writers—Elizabeth David, Jane Grigson, Elisabeth Luard, Nigel Slater—with no intention of cooking any of the recipes. (I am of the school of cuisine that believes you can eat well by learning how to shop.) I read and love these books not for instruction but for the sentences. For good food writing is, like all good writing, both precise and evocative.

When, in the early 1950s, Elizabeth David wanted to remind her ration-coupon British readers of the taste of figs, wild garlic and Kalamata olives, her sentences had to be as bright and unencumbered as the Mediterranean sun. Before the 1970s, it was hard to source the more exotic ingredients in her recipes outside of Soho delicatessens. For the metropolitan middle classes, her mentions of eggplants and anchovies were a partly vicarious pleasure, a reminder of the summers they were starting to spend in Tuscany and Provence. The best food writing walks this blurred line between sound advice and sensual reminiscence.

Provided you skip the dull bits about metric measures and oven settings, the sentences in a recipe are a pleasure to read. They are so sequential, so assured. *Warm two tablespoons of olive oil in a pan, then add the sliced onion.* The verdicts sound fair and true in a way that those in life rarely are. *Yesterday's bread has less moisture and so makes crisper toast.* Good food writing is clean, full of flavor, a meal in itself.

Elizabeth David wrote well, I suspect, because she saw what the culinary and writing arts have in common. A good sentence is the verbal fulfillment of her kitchen credo, borrowed from

Escoffier: *Faites simple*. She thought of good cooking as lucid and sincere—as a sentence should seem to be. She disliked rich sauces and other rococo effects that hid the true flavors of food. A sentence, too, should rely more on quality ingredients than baroque artifice. She frowned on kitchens weighed down with needless gizmos and other advertisements of culinary activity. A sentence, too, should not advertise the labor that went into its making. She hated English cooking that was a self-lacerating slog of peeling and boiling, when it should be an open-hearted labor of love. A sentence, too, should be—at least for the reader— an uncompromised joy.

•

If I were to write a pedant's apology, I think it would be, like Hardy's, a non-apology. In fact I think I would be less apologetic even than Hardy. He felt the need to justify the pointless beauty of a mathematical proof—the wholly non-utilitarian pleasure it brought to a small number of brilliant minds like his own. But most scientists now believe that beauty does have a point. When a theory looks too raggedy, they reach for Occam's razor, the principle of parsimony—after William of Occam, who held that "it is vain to do with more what can be done with less." They believe that an elegant equation is more likely to be right than an ugly one that seems to fit the data. Or rather they believe that natural symmetry and honed brevity are more likely to fit the data in the end.

Pleasing patterns play upon the brain's circuitry in ways that benefit the human tribe. We find pattern and symmetry pleasing in nature because it gives order and sense to the world. A palate finds pleasure in food as nerve endings find pleasure in sex. The pleasure they give profits the gene pool. Hardy's beloved prime numbers, the uselessness of which he saw as a virtue, turned out to have many uses—in electronics, computing and the Internet—that he could not have foreseen. Perhaps the pleasure of a beautiful sentence also allows our species to thrive in ways we cannot yet fathom.

At the start of the film *Broadcast News*, the young Aaron Altman (who grows up to be a smart and spiky journalist, played by Albert Brooks) is being beaten up in high school by the class bullies. As they hold him and hit him, he comes up with what he thinks is a devastating put-down: "You'll never make more than nineteen thousand dollars a year!" They throw him to the ground. He gets up and, his mouth full of blood, tries again: "You'll never leave South Boston and I'm going to see the whole damn world!" As they walk away laughing, he delivers his coup de grâce: "You'll never know the pleasure of writing a graceful sentence!"

Caring about how a sentence slots together can feel like a lonely and rarefied occupation. But Aaron Altman was right: it is worth the time it takes. Making a sentence sing is a way of making others more likely to listen and ourselves more likely to be understood. A good sentence gives order to our thoughts and takes us out of our solitudes. It is a cure, however fleeting, for human loneliness and for the chronic gulf of incomprehension that divides writer and reader, just as it divides any two of us.

And the cure is available to all, for free and without a prescription. Hardy was an impenitent elitist and thought it a waste of time doing math unless you were as gifted at it as he. But good writing is in reach of anyone, and all it asks for in return is the time it takes. I have used up much of my life on writing sentences, all of them effortfully made, most of them unbeautiful and quite a few unread. But I still think that time spent making them—even time spent deleting them furiously and then starting all over again—could never be a waste. I wrote this little book of sentences, a pedant's unapologetic apology, to say why.

2.

The Ape That Writes Sentences

Or why word order is (almost) everything

In 1979 Herbert Terrace, head of Columbia University's primate cognition laboratory, wrote an article for the journal *Science* titled "Can an Ape Create a Sentence?" For a scholarly paper, the answer was unusually emphatic: no.

Terrace and his colleagues had raised a chimpanzee, Nim Chimpsky, and taught him sign language. (For no ape can *speak* a sentence: their larynxes won't let them.) Nim was named, impishly, after Noam Chomsky, the ape-language skeptic who believed that humans alone were born with a universal grammar, a sort of sentence-generating implant in the brain. Terrace wanted to prove Noam wrong by teaching Nim to sign in sentences.

But after seven years of trying, Terrace decided that Nim had just learned to mimic his human teachers. He knew lots of words for things and could put them in basic permutations. He could say, "Tickle me Nim" or "Finish hug Nim" or "Apple eats Nim." But "Apple eats Nim" and "Nim eats apple" are not the same thing at all. Nim had failed to acquire a generative grammar, that human instinct for stringing words into sentences.

At the Great Ape Trust in Des Moines, Iowa, a bonobo chimp called Kanzi got a little further than Nim. Using a picture-symbol keyboard that voiced his words, he managed to pick up the proto-grammar of a two-year-old child. By fusing a noun and a verb into a two-word sentence, he could ask for M&Ms, burritos and orange soda. He could say he was "happy" or "sorry," use *to be* in its different forms and add the odd article and preposition. He could even sound sarcastic. Asked if he was ready, he would reply: "Past ready."

But Kanzi could not put words reliably in sentence order, or even identify that vital element, a subject. By the age of three, children have moved on from two-word nuggets and are spinning out intricate sentences that no one has ever said before. Lots of animals speak languages. But humans alone make these infinitely varied meanings out of a finite number of words and rules. Chomsky compared teaching apes syntax to teaching humans to fly. An Olympic long jumper, leaping thirty feet in the air, was not flying, he pointed out—and nor was an ape writing sentences.

Only human beings—for now, at least—make sentences. Like being able to make fire, or throw straight and true, or fall in love, no other animal can do it or wants to. Perhaps it all began, as Richard Dawkins has speculated, as a piece of brain software for collating our thoughts, which we later externalized as speech and then, eventually, writing. Whatever the cause, somewhere deep in our ancestral past we gained this knack for making sentences.

No ape can write a sentence, except the hairless one writing this one. Here I sit on this ergonomic swivel chair, my desk facing the wall so that I am not diverted from this ticklish and time-devouring task. We are stuck here, my brain and I, like roommates having to get used to each other's odd habits, until we have finished the job together. I may be better at writing sentences than a bonobo chimp, but it does not come easily to either of us. I tap away at the lettered keys, between long intervals staring at nothing. The taps complete an electrical circuit and the cursor moves rightwards, leaving a line of words behind. I am the ape that writes sentences, and so are you.

•

I teach in a university. I often wonder at all the writing going on in this place, the lines of words fed nonstop into the network, passing through fiber-optic cables, filling the ether or vaporizing into the electronic void, silent and invisible to all but their writer and one or two readers. On dark evenings, I walk past the glass-fronted library and see students tapping away inside this light-filled, open-plan space. All that mental toil going on in near silence, hidden in plain sight—and using up very little power, since someone told me that the computer memory needed for all the words our university produces in a day is smaller than that needed for one student streaming a single video clip. And yet words are what this place is for. A university is a factory where sentences are made.

Students come to the library shop floor to clock on for their shifts (unsupervised and irregular). They sit at the assembly line of computers making an accumulated sound, as they two-finger type, like soft spring rain pattering on the roof. Their predecessors printed out their writing and handed it in at counters in plastic pockets. But now it lives only on hard drives, memory sticks and the electronic submission systems of "virtual learning environments," where people like me read it and award it marks. All this writing has one thing in common. It consists of those little assemblages of words, separated by black dots, called sentences.

An English lecturer gets used to listening to laments about the younger generation's slide into illiteracy. I remain unconvinced. Of course, when marking essays I come across lots of bad sentences. The cut-and-shut jobs, which embark on a thought and then set off on another before the first is done with, until the end of the sentence has erased any memory of its beginning. The breathless run-ons: clauses just squashed together, needing full stops like lungs need air. The accidental fragments that, shorn of any sense of causation, read like bad haiku. The slow-motion car crashes, which start out fine until some slight syntactical wobble makes them career off the road, where the mangled syntax lies sprawling until the full stop ends its agony.

The ones with just too many needless words in them, stifling sense like knotweed.

But why do these bad sentences get written? Not because students are lazier or more illiterate than their forerunners, or less well taught. No, these sentences are bad because they stopped being visible and hearable to their writers. The writer knew what she wanted to say, thought she had said it, and gave up reading and listening. To write well you need to read and audit your own words, and that is a much stranger and more unnatural act than any of us know.

There is no evidence that people have gotten worse at writing sentences, and much evidence that they have always found it difficult. When the middle-aged and older complain that the young "can't even write a sentence," that exasperated adverb, *even*, implies that being able to write one is a kindergarten task, like learning to tie your shoelaces or recite your three times table. But writing a good sentence is hard—as hard, in its own way, as calculus. Even if you can get words in their basic order, you still have to put them in a way that moves, interests and charms the reader. To be able to write a sentence that someone else might read voluntarily and with pleasure is the work of a lifetime. I have been doing it for forty-odd years and sometimes I think I am getting the hang of it.

•

Of course I know that there are many things in life harder and more painful than writing a sentence. My point is only that everything is hard if done well. In Japan, where craftwork is seen as artwork, apprenticeships are long. A training in Bunraku puppetry, where three men work a single, half-human-sized puppet, lasts thirty years. The apprentice spends the first decade working the puppet's legs, the second one working the left arm, and the third working the right arm and the head, eyes and eyebrows. Only then may he be called a true master, his face now visible to the audience while those of his two accomplices stay hidden beneath black cowls.

A sushi master may make his apprentices wait years before they even touch the sushi. First they must sweep floors, learn to use their knives, and watch. Then they might just be allowed to dry some seaweed or massage an octopus until it is tender. A bonsai apprentice spends many seasons watering and feeding a tree before being permitted to prune it. An apprentice in *shodo* (calligraphy) takes years getting to know her bamboo-handled brushes, working over the top of her master's examples and perfecting her line—all for that moment when she consigns a few swift strokes to a hanging scroll.

What the Japanese call *shokunin katagi*, the artisanal spirit, is about much more than skill. It bears the social obligation to make something for the joy of making it, quietly and beautifully. It invests the simplest daily acts with artistry, whether it be making tea, raking Shirakawa gravel in a garden or curating that work of art and lunch that is a bento box. The point of life is to infuse the quotidian with the pleasure of creation and the pursuit of perfection.

The art of sentence craft seems ideally suited to this artisanal spirit. In a sentence, precision and grace go together. What matters is getting the little things right, for only through mastering these menial tasks do we find order and beauty. We learn to arrange and rearrange elements so that they fall just right on the eye of the beholder. And we discover the importance of beginnings, middles and endings. When Japanese children are taught to bow, they are told to punctuate the action with shape and meaning by pausing at the lowest point before coming back up. The Japanese turn life into art by making it a series of these short, graceful, self-contained gestures—like embodied and enacted sentences.

But there are no sentence masters, in Japan or anywhere else. We do not ask student writers to spend the first decade of their apprenticeship reading, before making them write sentences with just nouns and verbs, then letting them loose on modifiers, and only then, after many thousands of sentences, calling them *shokunin*, true artists of the craft. It is much easier instead to think that writing a sentence is easy. So we say that young people today "can't even write a sentence"—as if it were a basic skill without which no learning can begin, and not a lifelong task through which we can learn about life.

The best kinds of teaching pass on some usable splinter of knowledge, some stored-up wisdom of the tribe. A guitar chord, a sushi recipe, a bit of computer coding: it almost doesn't matter what. What matters is that you give it away, pass it on, pay it forward. Years ago a friend told me how to butter toast. Start buttering from the sides, she said, because enough ends up in the middle anyway. I have not seen that friend in a quarter of a century. But she was right, and every time I butter toast from the sides I thank her in my head.

I sometimes wish teaching were like this. In the humanities we train our students in new habits of thought, such as reading skeptically and thinking critically. We urge them to live with nuance and ambiguity. We set them off on the never-ending journey of interpretation, where they will have to weigh up unprovable notions that are, as the hard scientists say scornfully, "not even wrong." It may be useful but it can feel a little ... intangible.

Often I just want to say: this is what is wrong with this sentence and this is how to fix it. When I started marking essays, I felt wholly inadequate to this task. I made half-hearted efforts to untangle the knotted prose, but each untying seemed to reveal another knot, and a knot is always quicker to tie than to untie. All those jumbled-up tenses, subject–verb snarl-ups and absent or misapplied apostrophes. All that avoidable error reheated and served up again, then emended with the same red ink.

And all the time I knew that fixing a broken sentence is about so much more than just bandaging it up. In the margins I would write *Not a sentence!*—which is not a sentence either. That I, a teacher of English, could not do more to help my students made me feel feeble and fraudulent. I knew how to write sentences only by inkling or by accident; I did not have the wherewithal to explain to others what was wrong with theirs.

I wanted to show them how to make a line of thought out of words the way a vocal coach shows you how to make a sound out of breath, or the way my long-lost friend showed me how to make buttered toast out of butter and toast. If I could teach them that, I felt, they would take away a little piece of tribal wisdom, along with all those intangible things we try to teach them that aren't even wrong.

•

What I have learned is that trainee writers do not need to be able to parse every sentence into its parts. They just have to learn to *care*. Van Gogh, in a letter to his brother Theo, wrote that "what is done in love is well done." The purest form of love is just caring—paying someone else the compliment of your curiosity and holding them in your head, if only for a moment. The purest form of praise is to pay attention. This is how we offer up the simplest of blessings to the world around us and to the lives of others. "Attention," wrote the French thinker Simone Weil, "is the rarest and purest form of generosity." Give your sentences that courtesy and they will repay you.

I heard of a professor of art history at Harvard who told her students to go to a gallery and stand in front of the same painting for three hours, noting down their thoughts about it as they evolved. Her point was that three hours is a painful, even absurd, amount of time to look at a painting. Most gallery-goers glance at an exhibit for a few seconds, squint at the wall caption and walk away. It must break the hearts of any artists looking on.

But this professor's students had to dredge up unknown

reserves of patience if they were not to expire of boredom. They had to stand in front of the painting, as Rilke once wrote that he had learned to do with Cézanne's work, "more seeingly." They had to notice things they usually missed: that tiny wisp of cloud in the sky or a blurred face in a crowd, the shadow cast by an object, the brushwork, texture and stray drips of paint, the glaze veneer with all its gathered-up dust and grime, and the way the work lived amid the white space of wall around it, just as words on a page need white space around them to be read.

So now I say this to students. Find a sentence you like and look at it for a distressingly long time, until you start to see past its sense into its shape. As with a painting, the trick is not to exhume some buried symbolism or esoteric meaning, but only to make time to look. Take the sentence apart and reverse-engineer it, the way that computer programmers do when they dismantle software to see if they can copy it without infringing the rights. Turn its shape into a dough-cutter for your own sentences. Learn to love the feel of sentences, the arcs of anticipation and suspense, the balancing phrases, the wholesome little snap of the full stop.

Sometimes I read them bits of Jonathan Lethem's story "The King of Sentences." The young narrator and his girlfriend, Clea, work in a New York bookstore, worshipping sentences in books and reading them out to each other at night in bed—especially those of a reclusive writer they call "the King of Sentences." Every experience of theirs must be turned into sentences. When they find a sentence they like, such as "I said I want my eggs scrambled not destroyed," they scribble it on the wall of their apartment with a wax pencil. Or they type it out twenty-five times, then photocopy that page twenty-five times, then guillotine each page into twenty-five strips and scatter the strips through the streets for others to enjoy.

I don't tell the students the end of the story—the bit where Clea and the narrator track the King of Sentences down to a one-horse town upstate, and he takes his revenge by making them strip in a motel room, stealing their clothes and leaving them there, naked and ashamed.

•

Teaching English at the University of Kentucky in the 1980s, Wendell Berry set one of his graduate classes this assignment: write a single sentence. For another course, he relented, and let them write three sentences. In his essay "Standing by Words," Berry argues that the sentence is the indispensable tool with which we see, feel and know the world. "A sentence," he writes, "is both the opportunity and the limit of thought—what we have to think with, and what we have to think *in*."

Along with writing and teaching, Berry farms. Since moving back to his home state from New York in 1964, he has worked a few acres on a hillside in the bluegrass, overlooking the Kentucky River. Like most farmers he is unsentimental about nature, seeing it as something to wrestle with and work round. The purely natural and the purely human are to him equally undesirable states. There is nothing wrong with using nature for our own ends, so long as we see that we also have a duty to sustain it and must live within its limits.

A sentence, too, sits somewhere between the natural and the human. A writer must live within its limits. The sentence assiduously hews meaning out of the resistances of life and language. It is a little tussle with words and the world, and like farming it should never be done at the world's expense.

Berry believed in sustainability before it had a name. In 1965 he and his wife bought an electric stove and washing machine they still use. In 1973, when tractors and combines seemed to have vanquished horsepower for ever, he bought a team of sorrel mares to plow his fields. In 1987 he wrote an essay for *Harper's*, "Why I Am Not Going to Buy a Computer." One of his arguments for sticking with a pencil, and asking his wife to type up his drafts on the Royal Standard typewriter he bought new in 1956, was unorthodox: he felt that if he used a computer he would be in thrall to the big energy firms. "I would hate to think that my work as a writer could not be done without a direct dependence on strip-mined coal," he wrote. For similar reasons he wrote in the day, without electric light.

Making sentences with a pencil, in his little writer's hut next to the river, is, for Berry, a bit like farming. You ply your pencil rather as you guide a team of horses with harness and trace chains. Both require a steady yet supple hand. Put just enough pressure on the page and you come out with lines of words, rather as the plow draws its blade through soil and comes out with a line for planting seed.

Berry set his students that single-sentence assignment because he wanted them to slow down. He objected to the word processor precisely because it makes writing easier and faster. An office tool, a prisoner of urgency, it processes words quickly, just as a food processor blends leek and potatoes quickly into soup. We put the writing we do on computers into *files* and *documents*. The desktop computer was designed to serve the needs of the office memo and formula letter, not the desire to write things that others might read without being professionally obliged to do so. Its job was to accelerate the output of words. A rational aim in an office, perhaps, but not wherever words are meant to kindle curiosity, lift hearts and give others the courage to go on living.

There is no virtue in volume, no benefit in bulk. The world has plenty of sentences already, so pause before you add to the pile. Most of us, when we write, march too quickly on to the next sentence. To write intelligibly is hard enough, so be sure you have done that first. Fix your sights on making one sane, sound, serviceable sentence. As a farmer must do, hold your nerve and resist the impulse to put your energies into cash crops with quick returns. Have the confidence to leave fields fallow, to wait patiently for the grain to grow and to bear with the dry seasons.

At the end of a day's writing, you may find you have deleted more than you have inserted, and thus created something that is less than nothing. The computer makes this self-obliterating part of writing—cutting, pasting, typing, retyping, cutting again—alarmingly easy. It can feel like building an ornate sandcastle and then, before some beach bully does the job for you, stamping all over it yourself. When faced with such conspicuous failure, it is tempting to make do with something when you might be better off with nothing. Writing, just like farming, demands both patient work and stoic acceptance when that work comes to naught. The harvest is bountiful or it isn't; the sentences come or they don't—but eventually, always, they will.

There has been a recent vogue for applauding the lost virtues of slowness. Slow food, slow exercise, slow fashion, slow gardening, slow parenting, slow cities, slow science, slow cinema, slow television. These movements urge us to savor the sourcing and cooking of a meal, or watch a documentary composed only of the view through a train window on a long journey, or leave our children to explore the world unsupervised and at their own pace. In a fast world in pursuit of instant answers, slowness has become a dissident act. Perhaps a sentence slowly written, and slowly relished, could work in the same way, as a last redoubt against the glib articulacy of a distracted age.

•

In the 1980s Berry was far from being the only computer refusenik in the society of authors. He is almost alone in not recanting since (although we can guess what one of his great influences, Thoreau, a pencil-maker's son, would have made of Microsoft Word). I never had to recant because I was never a refusenik. When I started writing on a computer I felt at home right away in the hushed and liquefied space of the screen, with its winking cursor gently inviting me to have my say. Never did I look back longingly at typewriter paper smothered with correction fluid or screwed up in the bin. Nor, I confess, if I ever had to plow a field, would I bother with a dray horse if a tractor were available.

So I am no machine-wrecker. But part of me now wonders if technology does make things too easy, or rather makes them seem too easy. Perhaps, in the age of pinging alerts, status updates and other kinds of instant contact, we have been lured into thinking that it is simple to say what we mean and be understood.

Writing on a computer has a pretend polish, a deceiving veneer of finality. As soon as you type, it looks neatly justified, nattily formatted and halfway to being published. And that is even before the program has tidied up your spelling, spotted what it thinks are sentence fragments, scored your writing for "readability" and told you, with blithe, uninformed confidence, that you are done. *Spelling and grammar check complete. You're good to go!* Whatever its underlying condition, an onscreen sentence will scrub up as the finished article, like a smelly man in a sharp suit.

When you really wrestle with a sentence, and consider all the ways it can go wrong, you see that writing even a single one is a leap in the dark, with no assurance that it will land in a place that lets it make sense to someone else. Writing a sentence is slow and laborious whichever way you come at it. So labor-saving devices—like those salad tossers and egg slicers that claim to speed things up but actually just litter your kitchen—don't help much.

This, according to Verlyn Klinkenborg, is the lesson a writer learns most reluctantly of all. "It's necessary to write as if your sentences will be orphaned, because they will be," he writes. "When called to the stand in the court of meaning, your sentences will get no coaching from you. They'll say exactly what their words say, and if that makes you look ridiculous or confused, guess what?" Once our sentences are written and sent out into the world to be read, they are on their own. Most of us cling to a residual belief that we will still be there, hovering over the reader as she reads, to explain, when she stumbles over our words, what we really meant. We won't.

But our sentences are not quite orphans. What they really are is children with parents who love them but who can do nothing to help them. These parents are their writers. They are like the mothers and fathers who fret from the sidelines on school sports day as their child flunks the egg-and-spoon race, or who look on helplessly as he fluffs his single line in the end-of-year play. Parents may flush with mortification or pride at what their children do. But the flushing serves no purpose. That child is already a little self-directed bundle of flesh and blood. Like children, your sentences must sooner or later fly the nest. They will totter over the edge, blink into the abyss and, while you hold your breath, flap their wing-fluff and leap.

Writing a sentence is easy and it is hard. It is easy because words are the world's gift to us all, as free as light and air. And it is hard because you have to arrange them in such a way that they can be deciphered in your absence. In this sense, at least, the sentence writer is nothing like a sushi master. The robed *itamae* balletically slices his lozenge of tuna belly, sets it atop a rectangle of perfectly sticky rice smeared with wasabi paste, places it on a black-lacquered square, offers it up like a wet jewel and watches as you eat. This is not a meal; it is an exam, and both of you are being judged.

Writing is different. Once you have given your words up to be read, you are no longer there to await a response, and, as the French say, *Les absents ont toujours tort*. The absent—including the writer of these sentences you are reading, who has wisely made himself scarce—are always wrong.

Sentences that fail are a dialogue of the deaf. Reading one is like listening to someone in a nightclub over a pounding bassline. You can feel the writer's hot breath on your cheek but the words are muffled. All you end up with is an earful of broken syntax and spit. The sentence has not tried hard enough to reach the reader, or it has tried too hard and died in the attempt. It could shout at you for eternity and not give up its secrets. These are enduring laments about writing. The master of spoken dialogue, Socrates, worried away in Plato's *Phaedrus* at the willful deafness of written words. "They seem to talk to you as if they were intelligent," he said. "But if you ask them anything about what they say, from a desire to be instructed, they go on telling you just the same thing forever."

•

The word *sentence* has come to mean a verdict, a judgment from on high. This kind of sentence is the decisive end to a long deliberation. After the arrest, the trial, the guilty verdict and the pleas in mitigation comes the sentence—pronounced in open court, by a presiding judge, in front of the accused. Once the sentence has been passed, it must be carried out.

A written sentence is not like that at all. The word *sentence* comes from the Latin *sentire*, "to feel." A sentence must be felt, and a feeling is not the final word, but something that grows, ripens and fades like anything else that is alive. A line of words should unfold in space and time, not reveal itself all at once, for the simple reason that it cannot be read all at once. Out of this immovable fact about the sentence—it unfolds—flows everything else. As a sentence unfolds, it must feel alert and open to the world. The biologist Edward O. Wilson coined the word *biophilia*, "love of life," to describe the uniquely human trait of being drawn to everything that is vital and alive. We love a good sentence for biophiliac reasons: it breathes and moves like a living thing. It is words set in motion.

The anthropologist Tim Ingold has a theory that humans live, and give their lives meaning, by making lines. In a world of continual growth and movement—a world of life—lines are how we make it all cohere, how we hold things together within what would otherwise be a formless flux. "Every thing is a parliament of lines," Ingold writes. "To study both people and things is to study the lines they are made of."

Without the aid of lines we could not practice ancient crafts like weaving and rope-making, which depend on the threading and knotting of linear fibers. We could not join the stars up into constellations, or slice the world into latitude and longitude, or survey the land with trigonometry and theodolite. We could not plow a field and plant in rows, or walk along paths and roads, or fly, or sail across the sea. We could not paint, since the first thing an artist does is draw a line, nor read or write. Lines are how humans live, learn and make life up as they go along. A line, where a substance (such as ink) and a medium (such as paper) meet, lays down a trail of life. A sentence is a living line of words.

The branch of grammar that puts words into this living line is syntax. Inflected languages such as German and Latin depend less on word order. Wherever they are in the sentence, the subject and object are marked by their word endings. English has only a few such inflections. In an English sentence, word order is (almost) all.

We tend to think of words as the patterned tiles of the sentence, and syntax as the grout that glues them together and keeps them watertight. The first rule of sentence-making is that it works the other way round. Syntax is what brings the words to life and makes them move. The poet-critic Donald Davie had a nice phrase to describe its miraculous gift for breathing life into words just by putting them next to other words: "silent eloquence."

•

Only bad poets think that rules cramp their style. The good ones know that rules are the road to invention, that a cramped little corner with just enough legroom may be the best spot to consider the universe. Rules force us to plumb our brain's depths for the word that will fit the shape it needs to fit. They let us say things that are just beyond our imaginative reach and write over our own heads before we know quite what we are saying.

Syntax is like that: a marvel of organized flexibility, of restrained liberties and liberating restraints. It is a bit like those other traditional ways of binding things together, like building walls, weaving cloth or knotting rope. Through trial and error, our ancestors came up with ways of joining stuff together that are stout and steadfast, that cope with seas and storms and that have a simplicity that is its own kind of beauty.

Just as bridges and tall buildings are built to sway slightly in the wind and expand and shrink in the heat and cold, syntax's strength comes from its elasticity. Donald Barthelme's story "Sentence," itself a 2,000-word sentence, ends with an affirmation of this infinitely supple power: "the sentence itself is a man-made object, not the one we wanted of course, but still a construction of man, a structure to be treasured for its weakness, as opposed to the strength of stones."

As a boy I collected Legos. Merging my collection with that of my friends to undertake bigger construction projects, I remember thinking it impressive that each brick, whichever child it belonged to, slotted reliably into every other brick. For Lego is a global system. Each of the roughly 200 billion bricks made since 1963 will click into any other. The studs on top lock with the tubes beneath, without fail. Each brick is molded to tolerances of one hundredth of a millimeter, so they slide in nicely but sit tight, with the tensile strength of concrete. With these small cuboids you can make a whole mini-metropolis, a plastic Lilliput where Lego-figure groundlings pound the streets, work in offices, give birth in the hospitals and come to rest in cemeteries—all of it built one little brick at a time.

Syntax is not so different. The same basic elements—those virtual Lego bricks known as parts of speech—make endlessly varied shapes. The *Oxford English Dictionary* holds half a million words, a number that rises by about a thousand a year. However many words are made, they still snap together with the same force, so long as we learn how to snap them together well.

A classic way to do this is time, manner and place. It is there in Old English, in the stout sentences of the tenth-century monk-scholar Aelfric, which say what someone did, when, how and where: "This aforesaid holy man was wonted that he would go at night to the sea and stand on the salt brim up to his neck, singing his beads." Stick to time, manner and place and your sentence will never seem cluttered. For you will be relaying an unbroken action in the world of linear time and three-dimensional space within which all of us are stuck. *In the early hours I took off my shoes and crept into the spare room. That night I slept fitfully on an inflatable bed. The next day I rose late and went downstairs with a sheepish look.*

•

In 1984 two New York computer programmers, William Chamberlain and Thomas Etter, published a book of poems and short pieces called *The Policeman's Beard Is Half Constructed.* It was written by a prose-synthesis program they had devised called Racter, short for *raconteur.* Racter arranged its 2,800-word vocabulary according to "syntax directives." By conjugating verbs, remembering genders and matching pronouns, it could do something no bonobo chimp could do: make sentences out of words.

These sentences were semantically surreal but syntactically flawless. Racter could sort its stack of words into a dry parody of scholarly method. *This dissertation will show that the love of a man and a woman is not the love of steak and lettuce.* Or it could work up a tone that nestled somewhere between flirtation and insult. *I was thinking as you entered the room just now how slyly your requirements are manifested.* Or it could join sentences together into wild, wondrous cadences. *Bill sings to Sarah. Sarah sings to Bill. Perhaps they will do other dangerous things together. They may eat lamb or stroke each other. They may chant of their difficulties and their happiness. They have love but they also have typewriters. That is interesting.*

Racter sounded both gently wise and gently insane. Its sentences made little sense, but nor were they nonsense. They seemed to have been written by a human who was also a part-time alien. Nothing was being said and yet everything was, the serendipity of word order having given birth to a fragile profundity. Racter wrote better than many human writers because it did not allow jumbled thought or intruding ego to get in the way of what it wanted to say. The word order took most of the weight.

The force of Racter's prose relied on one basic truth. A sentence, as it proceeds, is a gradual paring away of options. Each added word, because of English's reliance on word order, reduces the writer's alternatives and narrows the reader's expectations. Yet even up to the last word the writer has choices and can throw in a curveball. A sentence can begin in one place and end in another galaxy, without breaking a single grammatical rule. The poet Wayne Koestenbaum calls it "organizing lava," this pleasure to be got from "pushing a sentence in a wrong direction without altering its sweet grammatical composure."

Racter's lesson for the sentence writer is never to say everything. If you make the familiar shape of a sentence, it will remind the reader of meaning. We take our reading cues from syntax, so when the words fill the right slots, we cannot help but shape them into sense and imagine the world they suggest. Leave bits of silence, unsaid words between your actual words and gravid pauses between your sentences. Amid these gaps, implications sit. If you resist spelling it all out, the rhythm of the words makes its own eerie sense. A sentence must say something, but it can be a half-said thing and the better for it. It can floor you like a Zen koan and still have its own kind of clarity.

Fairy tales, Angela Carter once wrote, are like potato soup. When we make potato soup, or retell a fairy tale, we are putting our own spin on an old domestic art, passed down, with lots of edits and add-ons, into the present. There is no official recipe and no copyright. No one owns the recipe for a sentence either.

That neat bit of open-source software, syntax, lets us tap into a vast shared wisdom about how words best join together, and devise word orders that feel right and that make us sound wise.

Writing a sentence is a way of withdrawing intelligence for free from this syntactical cashpoint that never runs empty. Good writers are not always shrewder or more sagacious than the rest of us. Mostly they have just found a better way of withdrawing from the ATM and sounding wiser than they are. Didn't Racter sound wry and penetrating, even if it was neither? So can you, even if you are neither.

"As I altered my syntax," W. B. Yeats wrote, "I altered my intellect." Most skilled writers see writing this way, less as a form of self-expression than as a way of releasing them from the confused and faltering self they usually present to others. Writing, Kurt Vonnegut once said, allows "mediocre people who are patient and industrious to revise their stupidity, to edit themselves into something like intelligence." Making even one good sentence may be hard, but it is worth it—just to edit our thoughts into fluent intelligence, to build a ladder of words up to our better selves.

•

The written sentence never needed to exist. Every human tribe has worked out how to commune using the shaped and sculpted breath of the voice. Only a few, and only in the last few thousand years, have set words down in writing. The first writing, by the Sumerians on the Mesopotamian plain, was just for recording quantities of corn, oil or cattle. The true heir of those little clay tablets is not the sentence but the spreadsheet.

Many cultures have got by with this kind of partial script, instead of a full script, like cuneiform or Latin, that can be used to write epic poetry as well as to count corn—that can be wrought, in other words, into sentences. Whole civilizations, full of rich ways of speaking their loves and fears and revulsions, have risen and fallen without writing a single word.

Some dieticians think that gluten intolerance is common among humans because our digestive tracts have had just a short period in our long evolution to get used to it. Our ancestors started to turn wheat into bread only a few thousand years ago. Which one of them first had this unobvious idea? Whoever it was, they had to think this: that it might be quite a good idea if we grew some wheat, dried it, ground it into flour, mixed it with oil, water and yeast to make dough, kneaded it into a ball, waited for it to rise, baked it until it looked brown and sounded hollow, and then ate it. Perhaps some hunter-gatherer left his grainy gruel on a hot rock near the fire and inspiration struck. But making bread is still ingenious—so ingenious, perhaps, that our stomachs have yet to catch up with its ingenuity.

Could the same be true of sentences? As a species we are new to this game—and a sentence is a far stranger and more contrived thing even than bread. It asks us to go off alone and make marks on a page or screen, which may at some point in the future be seen by absent others. It wants us to believe in its power to mean something to persons unknown and elsewhere, perhaps even after our own life is over. Hardly surprising that we are still getting used to this odd, lonely act, and that even after years of schooling in it, we still flounder.

In writing, meaning derives from just four things: syntax, word choice, punctuation and typography. These four things, in that order of importance, must stand in for the unique print of a human voice. They do the work of all those tiny variations in pitch and inflection that let us identify someone we know, even over a dodgy phone line, from their first *hello*. When that person is in front of us, we have even more to go on: smiles, scowls, eyebrow lifts, eyelid drops, the bulk of a proximate human body. A writer has just scratches on paper, or pixels on a screen.

Most of what comes out of our mouths is not sentences. The spoken word stops dead in mid-thought, self-corrects, starts again and then falls away with no full stop. Speech is full of waste. The listener just sifts out the filler words or uses them as pauses for deciphering sense. But if they turn up in writing they feel to a reader like word fuzz. They don't kill the meaning but they bore and grate, like the hiss and wheeze of radio static.

We know that Homer's epics were first spoken, because they are full of such hand-me-down, repeated phrases like *when they had put away their desire for food and drink* or *and so she said when smiling.* In Homer the heavens are *starry* even in daylight. Achilles is *swift-footed* even when sulking in his tent. The dawn is *rosy-fingered* in all weathers. Without these stock brick words, Homer (or, more likely, several Homers) could not have extemporized aloud while still obeying the stern demands of classical hexameter. The ancient art of rhetoric needed such ready-mades, stored in the mind to ensure *copia*, or fluent abundance, in speech.

The earliest writing was different. Some of it took the form of epigrams engraved on the bases of Greek tombs. Samples survive from the eighth century B.C.E. The traveler in antiquity saw them often by the roadside, as familiar a sight as road signs. Here they ventriloquized the dead man, addressing the passerby with some clipped meditation on mortality. Their most famed exponent was Simonides of Ceos, who in the fifth century B.C.E. wrote lines honoring the dead of the Persian wars. *We did not flinch but gave our lives to save Greece when her fate hung on a razor's edge.* Stone offered scant space and an unforgiving writing surface, which urged brevity. Epigrams had to be literally lapidary, incisive in the first sense of the word. *Stranger, tell the Spartans that we lie here, obedient to their words.*

So the earliest epigrams—the earliest sentences—were epitaphs, marking a death. A good sentence on a bleak theme can be oddly cheering. To clothe despair in eloquence is to show that it can be endured. The sentence moves inevitably toward and then marks its own demise, with a full stop. It suggests that anything can be borne, even one's own passing, and that a meaningful life knows how sure is its end. A well-written sentence acts as an antidote to self-pity and banality. It may say something obvious—this person died, as we all will—without sliding into cliché or cant. Or it may say something unobvious that, once said, seems true forever.

•

Carved letters are three-dimensional things, which alter with the angle of vision and the light. Their solid, enduring form gives them a special kind of serenity. The great English letter-carver David Kindersley told his apprentices as they gathered each day in his workshop: "We are going to make something beautiful, appropriate, something that adds to the world." Kindersley, like his mentor Eric Gill, wanted to revive the status of letter-carving as an art. Letter-carvers had once been seen as artists, like painters and sculptors, but now they were looked on as mere artisans, like printers. Writers, meanwhile, had come to be seen as intellectuals or creative people, working with the mind, not as scribes, working with the hands.

It helps, I think, to keep hold of something of that older sense of the writer as a carver of sentences. Consider the sentence as a crafted object that will take up space in three dimensions. Look at it as a letter-carver must, knowing that each chip of chisel on stone is hard-won and immutable. See it as something that will add to the world. It may remind you to make each word count.

In his book *The Hare with Amber Eyes*, Edmund de Waal relates the journey made by 264 *netsuke*—small Japanese ivory or wood carvings—which came circuitously into his possession after his ancestors had their estate seized by the Nazis. At the start of the book de Waal rolls one of the *netsuke* round his palm and fingers. As a craftsman himself, a potter, he marvels at its artistry, down to the tiny signature of the maker on the sole of a sandal. The *netsuke*, he writes, is "a small, tough explosion of exactitude" that "displaces a small part of the world around it." Not a bad description either of the crystalline brevity of a good sentence: a small explosion of exactitude.

•

In the ancient world, the epigram migrated from stone to papyrus and became an art form. A poet could make a living as an *epigrammatopoios*, or epigram fashioner. One such was Callimachus, librarian at the Great Library of Alexandria in the third century B.C.E. His epigram on the death of his friend Heraclitus begins with an expertly sprung, note-perfect sentence. *Someone told me of your death, Heraclitus, and it moved me to tears, when I remembered how often the sun set on our talking.*

The sprawling epic and the sparse epigram were the rival literary forms of antiquity. Virgil and Ovid cleansed their palates between epics by turning epigrams. Callimachus's all-purpose put-down was *big book, big bore* (itself a model of brevity, with no need even of a verb). In the first century C.E., the satirist Martial perfected a generic refinement: a switchblade, puncturing twist in the last few words. Writers were learning that a sentence wields more power with a strong stress at the end, where it stays in the mind and sends a backwash over the words that went before.

The epigram grew into a container for any occasion: birthday salutations, wine tasting, a young man's first shave, victories in chariot races, little digs at esteemed figures like doctors or athletes. Now it appeared on objects other than tombs, like this epigram of Martial's engraved on a bedroom lantern: *A lamp am I, aware of your joy in bed: Do what you will, not one word will be said.* Each sentence gave a voice to the thing on which it was written, like those hokey-friendly notes written nowadays on bagged salads and smoothie bottles. *Keep me in the fridge and shake me before pouring. Wash me thoroughly.*

The epigram taught the ancients how to turn a sentence, how to enclose a little world of meaning in a line of words. The defining quality is the removal of redundancy. A sentence, like an epigram, says the most it can with the scarcest resources. We see the same idea at work in the clean lines of a Shaker table or a Federer forehand. Beauty, this ancient artistic law has it, derives from economy. A writer should dread "surplusage," Walter Pater wrote, as the runner should dread it on his muscles. Students come and tell me that their essay is over-length and they can't make it any shorter. I reply, as gently as I can because I have felt just as attached to my words, that they need to try harder.

•

For a sentence-maker, the epigram remains excellent training. One of its great modern practitioners was the Scottish artist Ian Hamilton Finlay. Finlay started out as a writer but came to reject consecutive sentences in favor of the aphorism, which he called the philosopher's "hand-grenade." He turned to conceptual art, collaborating with sculptors, potters, glassmakers and sign-writers. They helped him to solidify his sentences. His words were now embroidered on fabric, lit in neon, sandblasted in glass, printed on silk screen and cut into stone and slate at his garden in the Lanarkshire hills. *The smaller the country the larger the stamps. He who lives alone is always on sentry duty. When our friends leave us, they take away our shores.*

One of Hamilton Finlay's last exhibitions, in Edinburgh in 2005, was simply titled "Sentences." All the exhibits were mono-stichs, one-sentence poems, painted in different colors on the white walls, like bright-tinted spells. *Thinking assumes settled weather. Too much chatter sprains the soul. The Late Night Shipping Forecast is a kind of High Church Weather Service for radio listeners. Stupidity reduces language to words.* These sentences, like all good epigrams, sounded intimate yet impersonal, as if a voice were addressing the reader warmly from a distance. They were private admissions with the power of public utterance—a secret conversation with humanity, one human at a time.

The epigram is enjoying a resurgence as public art. Jenny Holzer started it all in the late 1970s, wheat-pasting posters of lithographed "truisms" to walls and telephone booths in New York. *Abuse of power comes as no surprise. There's nothing redeeming in toil.* Written large in lights above Times Square in 1982, competing with the illuminated ads for Panasonic and Coca-Cola, were her words *Protect me from what I want*—a plea, perhaps, to be saved from the banal addictions of consumerism. Holzer now makes LED light pieces that speed her oracular sentences through galleries in bursts of digital wordage. Moving up, down and across, the words vanish as they hit the base or edge of a wall, as if sliding under or through it.

The people you love become ghosts inside of you and like this you keep them alive. The artist Robert Montgomery wrote that sentence after a friend from art college was hit by a car and killed. He turned it into a light piece, lit by recycled sunlight and erected on the promenade on London's South Bank, like an off-beam Blackpool illumination. Outside Baptist churches, aping those evangelical signs that say *You are never too lost to be saved* or *God loves you whether you like it or not*, Montgomery displayed his own sign: *God is bored of us.* He spent five days on top of a soon-to-be-demolished multistory car park in Cardiff putting up a single sentence in ten-foot-high backlit aluminum: *All Palaces are Temporary Palaces.*

Londoners who keep their eyes open will have noticed the work of Martin Firrell, another artist who likes to hijack public spaces for stealthily subversive declarations. His sentences have filled the giant screen in Leicester Square, the lightbox signs outside Curzon cinemas and the dome of St. Paul's Cathedral. He used to be a copywriter and his words read like ad slogans gone off-message. *Protest is liberty's ally. Aging is a privilege, not a predicament. Learn to love rain.*

When writing a sentence, I sometimes ask how it would stand up as this kind of text art. What would this one look like, I wonder, signed in electric light at Piccadilly Circus, or rushing in a ticker-tape stream across a white wall at Tate Modern? You might think me presumptuous, imagining my words being pored over by sightseers or by hushed gallery-goers earnestly seeking meaning. But so much writing is just ambient word static, typographic white noise. Picture your sentence up in lights, a stack of words staring straight back at you, demanding thought, and it focuses the mind. Some people find text art pretentious (as can I, sometimes). But at least a sentence blown up on a wall has stood up to be counted. Writing exists not to be wasted on the air like speech, but to be committed to permanence. A sentence should warrant its arrival into the world.

The bastard child of the epigram is today's favorite literary form, the inspirational quote. The fortune-cookie philosophy once confined to fortune cookies is now everywhere, scattered a quote per page in bathroom books and pasted on to JPEGs, with a seascape as background and a picture of the quote's alleged author with a faraway look. *Goals are just dreams with deadlines. We only regret the chances we didn't take. If you're brave enough to say good-bye, life will reward you with a new hello.*

These are the heirs of the spare lines of a Simonides or Callimachus. No longer etched on roadside stones or wax tablets, they are sent off in little electronic packets through the Web, to be shared, favorited and forgotten. Wherein lies their appeal, albeit as short-lived as a sugar rush? They also are sentences.

•

To write a sentence you will need the following. First, some words. Second, a feel for how those words might fit together. Third, a writing tool and surface, some implement and conveyance for turning your words into a visible form that allows them to be tipped into someone else's brain. Last, the thing that people forget they need: a memory.

A short-term memory retains stuff in your head for about half a minute. Without it, language is impossible, because to understand a sentence a listener or reader has to remember the start until the end. The curse of the Struldbruggs, the immortals who live on the isle of Luggnagg in *Gulliver's Travels*, is that they cannot occupy themselves in eternity with reading, because their memories "will not serve to carry them from the Beginning of a Sentence to the End."

You cannot read a sentence without this working memory that keeps the whole thing in your head until the full stop closes the loop. Reading a sentence is like juggling words, throwing them up in the air until they come to rest. If the sentence is too convoluted, the reader is throwing up too many things—billiard balls, wooden clubs, burning torches—while standing on a balance board. One thing ends up being dropped and then it all comes clattering down.

In 1986 David Snowdon, a young epidemiologist at the University of Minnesota, stumbled upon this problem of language and memory when he visited a nearby convent run by the School Sisters of Notre Dame. Many of the nuns were in their eighties and nineties. He found some of them fit and well, cheering at the baseball on TV or working out in the gym. Others were in the sickbay, slumped in wheelchairs and silently fingering rosaries. Snowdon had the idea that nuns would make an ideal control group for a study of Alzheimer's. Nuns from the same order have the same diet, health care and fitness regime all their adult lives. The data is unclouded by variables. Snowdon enlisted 678 elderly nuns and launched the "Nun Study."

With his colleague Susan Kemper, Snowdon compared personal essays that the elderly nuns at a Milwaukee convent had written in the 1930s, just before they took their vows. The nuns had followed the same writing brief in strikingly original ways. Their sentences read, to borrow a phrase from Marianne Moore, as "radiographs of personality." Snowdon and Kemper noted a contrast between the "high-fidelity" writers and the "listers." A high-fidelity writer wrote: "Now I am wandering about in Dove's

Lane waiting, yet only three more weeks, to follow in the footprints of my Spouse, bound to Him by the Holy Vows of Poverty, Chastity and Obedience." A lister wrote: "I prefer teaching music to any other profession."

Both these sentences are grammatical. One reader might prefer the former's intricacy, another the latter's plainness. But the first could only be written, not spoken, and the second is simple enough to be both. Now, sixty years on, the nun who wrote the first sentence was mentally sharp; the one who wrote the second had died of dementia. Those with rich styles seemed to be less at risk of dementia than those with listing styles. Even as novices, the nuns who would later get dementia had poorer working memories. Either Alzheimer's is a lifelong disease that grows slowly and manifests late, or a good working memory confers resistance to it just as reserves of calcium stave off arthritis. To write a sentence, you need a working memory, to keep the parts in play until they fall into place.

A sentence must stick in the mind. It has to be literally memorable, never so intricate that it cannot be absorbed all at once. I prefer to cast the whole sentence in my head before I set it down, and only if I get stuck do I surrender and rough it out in writing. If I can hold it all in my brain, my thinking goes, so can a reader. Michael Donaghy made a point of reciting his poems from memory at readings, on the grounds that if he could not remember them, he could hardly expect anyone else to. If you can think the sentence before you write it, it will be sufficiently uncontorted to slip into the reader's brain at first time of asking.

The limit of a spoken sentence is the breath capacity of our lungs. The limit of a written one is the memory capacity of our brains. The full stop at the end of a sentence sets the limit. By the time it arrives, you must still be able to recall the sentence's beginning. If you can't keep it all in your head, then maybe those words weren't meant to be together.

•

You have to hold the sentence in your head, but for it to be held in the reader's head as well, you must also write it down. And when you have done that you can see it, and tinker with it in ways that can't be done in the head. Now you can begin to work that unwieldy substance, words, like an artisan. Your sentences have turned from brain food into something to be molded with the tools to hand. A carver has a chisel and a lump of stone. A potter has a wheel and a lump of clay. A writer has a keyboard and a screen.

You like playing around with fonts, don't you? Switching serif to sans serif, toying with Garamond before coming home to Verdana, blowing the type up to 16 point and back down again? To a hostile witness, it might look as if you are doing unpaid typesetting as a displacement activity, the digital version of doodling in the margin. You are not. You are making your writing visible to yourself, because it keeps slipping into invisibility, enveloped by the mists of habit and inattention. You think you know what you have said and have become half-blind to what the words actually say. All your tritenesses and opacities have shrunk from view. Making your words visible again lets you see them again.

You are also trying to see how the words sit on the page or screen, because that will most likely be their only route to the reader. Typographers know that typefaces can shift the whole tone of a piece of writing (although for all the white magic they perform, they will never rescue a bad sentence). No matter how well they sound in your own head, the words must come to your reader through her own eyes.

•

Your aim is to clear a path for the reader, a way through the sentence that will not get her lost. In the field of human sentence-processing, scientists study what happens to our brains when we read sentences. They can track a reader's eyes and scan her brain as she reads a sentence, and spot where she pauses or backpedals as she mulls over its meaning. They are looking for evidence of those little syntactical traps in prose, moments of murk where the eye flickers and the brain stutters. Linguists call them *garden paths* because they lead the reader up them.

A sentence can confuse in countless ways. The smallest words, the ones that novice writers pay the least mind to, cause the biggest confusions. Prepositions confuse because they so easily shapeshift into conjunctions or adverbs in the reader's head. A poorly placed *for* or *as* is enough to lead the reader astray. *Since* can mean "because" but also "after that time." *While* can mean "although" but also "during that time." Prepositional phrases confuse if they are too far away from what they modify. *I wrote my speech while flying to Paris on the back of a sick bag.* Even over-correctness confuses. When you strain to avoid splitting an infinitive, believing (wrongly) that splitting one is wrong, it can draw attention to itself and give the reader pause.

Words make little sense outside of sentences. Philosophers focus so much on the sentence—a logician might spend years musing on the meanings of *is*—because it is the one place where words really mean anything. A word comes alive only as a part of speech; parts of speech live only in sentences. *I can swim in the river. I can peas in the factory.* Without sentences, words are rudderless rafts, stranded in an ocean of unmeaning with no land in sight.

No writer should delay the reader for no reason. If you stop the eye and check the reader's pace, there must be something worth seeing. If she is driven back to the start of the sentence to double-check a pronoun's antecedent or to work out which meaning of *as* or *with* you meant, then she has been waylaid into helping the writer do the writing. Such sentences are, like self-assembly furniture, unpaid labor. They are a pile of raw materials that the consumer has been duped into throwing together because it suits the producer's business model. The reader should not be asked to do the equivalent of lining up all the screws and dowels and puzzling over the instructions, only to find out that the Allen key is missing.

But a little confusion is fine, if it is quickly over. A team of neuroscientists at the University of Liverpool scanned the brains of volunteers, using nodes strapped to their heads, as they read Shakespeare in its original and in simpler form. The aim was to see how readers coped with his habit of jumbling up parts of speech. They found that a phrase like "him have you madded" excited the brain in a way that "you have enraged him" did not. Readers seemed to like sentences that bent the rules without breaking them. When the brain sees a phrase like "I could out-tongue your griefs," it pauses, puzzled, then assents to its distortions. We want a sentence to be clear but not too clear, odd but not off-puttingly so, so that it can catch us off-guard and remind us that we are alive.

A sentence writer is like a close-up magician, working with words instead of a deck of cards. Card magicians distinguish between sleights of hand and flourishes. Sleights of hand are the seemingly innocent gestures with which they manipulate the cards. They are the part the magician works hardest on but never wants us to notice. Flourishes are the fancy cuts, riffle shuffles, thumb fans and finger twirls. They are more like dancing than magic and, like a dance, are meant to be seen.

Some card magicians frown on flourishes because they underscore the magician's skill and show that the magic is not real. Others approve of them because they show that the magic comes from skill, not a trick deck. But all agree: a flourish should be visible, a sleight of hand not. A magician's task is to direct the gaze, to decide what the audience lingers on. The same goes for the writer. Anything that slows the reader down must be a flourish, not a sleight of hand gone wrong. Showing off only works if it is shored up by invisible labor. A sentence covers most, not quite all, of its tracks.

•

Writing is as driven by egotistical noise-making as any other human act. But in the end it should be an act of generosity, a gift from writer to reader. As with all gifts, giver and receiver must cut each other some slack. A sentence, before it can be made sense of, must be unraveled like a gift being unwrapped. The unraveling—fingernailing the sticky tape, tearing the paper, making sure the gift is the right way up so you can look suitably surprised and grateful as it emerges—should never feel like more trouble than it is worth. A gift given for self-centered reasons will try the givee's patience, because it will take up his time and still demand gratitude. But the givee is willing to do a little work, so long as it feels useful and involves no heavy lifting. He may not even mind if what is unwrapped is not quite what he wanted, so long as he enjoyed the unwrapping and the gift was given with a good heart.

A lot of writing wants you to know the effort that went into it. The gift of knowledge that a sentence contains should never have to be bought, as it often is, with the reader's boredom or confusion. Thoreau wrote in his journal that a sentence must have a weight of work behind it, yet show no strain and be "uttered with your back to the wall." In *Walden* he faithfully records the hours he spent at his log cabin observing woodchucks, red squirrels and tribes of warring ants, but never the much longer time he spent with his pencil, sharpening sentences.

In his book *The Gift*, Lewis Hyde argues that the driving force of human civilization has been the giving of gifts. The gift economies of remote tribal societies worked by constant circulation. The seafaring peoples of the western Pacific made long, perilous boat trips to other islands to exchange *kula*: bracelets and necklaces made of shells. They treasured these trinkets, which had little intrinsic worth, because of the network of relations they symbolized as they moved round the ring of islands. A commodity loses value if it is secondhand, but a certain kind of gift gains value the more hands that have held it. This kind of gift can never be stockpiled or sold, but must be constantly given away. "To have painted a painting does not empty the vessel out of which the paintings come," Hyde writes. "On the contrary, it is the talent which is not in use that is lost or atrophies, and to bestow one of our creations is the surest way to invoke the next."

The sentence is just such a gift. It takes something from the tribe—words, syntax, musical rhythm, templates of good sentences to emulate and surpass. It makes something of these materials, gives it back to the tribe, and the tribe gives it on to others. Like all true gifts, the sentence is the one that keeps on giving.

3.

Nouns versus Verbs

Or how to bring a sentence to life, but not too much

On 10 December 1941, three days after the Japanese attack on Pearl Harbor, a troubled and truth-seeking young man called Thomas Merton entered the Abbey of Gethsemani, a monastery in the wooded Appalachian hills near Louisville, Kentucky. Gethsemani was home to the most austere Benedictine order, the Cistercians of the Strictest Observance, or Trappists. Here Merton was to spend the next twenty-seven years—the rest of his life. The Gethsemani monks were forbidden to speak, except to superiors. They could use sign language, but only if it related to God, work or food. Those who made "noise" were named in the chapter of faults. In this world of little speech, Merton gave his life to writing.

He was allowed just a couple of hours a day in the scriptorium, and ordered to spend much of that time on Latin translations and pious lives of dead monks. When he did find time for his own writing, it had to get past the Cistercian censors. And yet, with all these obstacles, words poured out of him. He wrote over sixty books and hundreds of articles, talks, poems, and a journal that ran to over a million words. With so little time to write, he wasted no words on preambles and moved unfussily through his thoughts, in clear, necessary-seeming sentences. He spoke so little that writing became his way of talking to the world.

•

Merton knew that the hardest trick for any writer to pull off is to be clear without being glib or dull. He hated what he called "mere verbalizing," an unreal language cut off from the hard data collected by the senses. All Western thought since Plato, he felt, had fallen for this trap of thinking that abstraction was the highest form of thought. Not that one could ever do away with abstractions, because the fog of the world could never quite be bottled in words. A writer, he felt, made only sporadic "raids on the unspeakable."

Like all the Gethsemani monks, Merton lived both an intensely abstract and an intensely concrete existence. He spent his days thinking about the biggest questions of life and death, but he also met the world in the raw. He slept on a straw mattress with bare boards, ate a spartan vegetarian diet and rose in the dead of each night to sing the night office. Each day he put in six hours' hard labor digging up briars, threshing the alfalfa or chopping trees for the furnace. He knew enough of hunger to sweetly anticipate and slowly enjoy eating a simple chunk of sourdough bread dipped in blackberry juice.

In a world without central heating or air conditioning, Merton felt starkly the shifts in the seasons. In winter the bristles in his nose froze; in summer his woolen robes drenched him in sweat. He saw the sun rise each day, went to bed when it set and was ever alert to how its daily arc changed the light, hour by hour. He loved the dark, especially in the calm of Mass before dawn in the novitiate chapel. And he grew to love rain, especially on the fire watch, the nightly patrols the monks made to guard against fire, when a downpour would break the silence like an aviary full of prattling birds.

In November 1960, Merton's abbot gave him permission to spend some of his time at a hermitage, a breeze-block hut in the woods half a mile from the monastery. One of his loveliest pieces, "Rain and the Rhinoceros," came out of listening to the rain falling on the flat roof of his hut. In the town, he reflected, rain is what we hurry through with a newspaper over our heads while bearing the load of our solipsistic preoccupations. It has no worth in a world where anything of value must be measured, costed and consumed.

Rain—without which crops would die, rivers silt up and the world wizen into an endless Sahara—has become a mere abstraction, an innocuous conversation filler, a small tedium to ignore. In the woods, though, rain must be heeded. Here the noise and light of modern life cannot drown out its unrelenting rhythms or its wet, renewing sparkle.

Merton felt that by chasing after scarce goods that could not be shared by all, like money, rank and status, we ignored the free gifts around us. Rain, a gift from the skies, asked only that we stop and listen to it. "What a thing it is to sit absolutely alone, in the forest, at night," he wrote, "cherished by this wonderful, unintelligible, perfectly innocent speech, the most comforting speech in the world, the talk that rain makes by itself all over the ridges, and the talk of the watercourses everywhere in the hollows."

•

Rain is an interesting noun. It describes something real: actual beads of water falling to the earth, soaking clothes, swelling rivers, flooding roads and dotting pavements with puddles. But *rain* is also an abstraction. The word conflates all the different kinds of water that fall down on us, from cloudbursts to set-in rain to that floating dampness known as mizzle. And rain changes as it falls, so these subcategories can merge invisibly into each other—a reminder that *rain* is also a verb.

Rain can be an idea, an intimation: a dark cloud overhead *looks like rain.* Or it can be a general state: *The rain lasted all day.* Hedge funds trade in weather derivatives, allowing firms to protect themselves against the financial losses incurred by the rain that is always on the horizon, but unpredictably so. *Rain* is a wet certainty and a vague possibility. It feels more real than *precipitation*, but less so than *drizzle* or *downpour*, which carry the very droplets in their sounds.

A child learning to speak is learning nouns. *Mama, dada, doggie, juice, milk.* Early humans must have said their first words when their simian grunts turned into the names of things on the African plains at which they could point. Linguists talk about ultra-conserved words, ones so alike in so many languages that our common ancestors must have used them. Apart from the heartening verb *give,* they are nouns: *I, we, hand, star, fire, man.*

Our first instinct with words is to label and sort. That is how we get a fix on the world in a foreign tongue, learning the names for things and waving at them hopefully. Only later do we see that the world is not so easily pinned down, and that everything bleeds into everything else. For this we need verbs. Later still we give nouns not to things but to states with no material presence in the world, like *bliss* or *regret.*

Style guides often advise us to avoid these abstract nouns. They steer us instead toward concrete nouns that refer to things that at least one of our senses can grasp. Concrete nouns form pictures in our minds and evoke what can be felt, smelled, touched or tasted. The more particularizing a noun is—the more it calls to mind the noise, touch and tang of life—the closer it brings us to the world.

In his book *The Crofter and the Laird,* the American author John McPhee journeys to Colonsay, the tiny Hebridean island that was the home of his ancestors. Here, he discovers, "almost every rise of ground, every beach, field, cliff, gully, cave, and skerry has a name." The island has only 138 inhabitants, but 1,600 place names. Among them are *The Glen of the Baglike Plain, The Shelter of the Miserable Women, Bald Kenneth's Daughter's Fishing Rock* and *The Ruins of the House of Boisterous Angus.* These deeply precise names, McPhee writes, "sketch the land in language."

In 2007, when a new edition of the *Oxford Junior Dictionary* appeared, it emerged that fifty-odd nature words, including *bluebell, buttercup, catkin, conker* and *cowslip,* had been cut. They had made way for words like *chatroom, voicemail, phobia, therapy* and *celebrity*. Five years later a group of writers petitioned the publishers to reinstate the old words in a new edition, but to no avail.

Blaming dictionary makers for language use might feel like blaming weather forecasters for the rain. But these writers were surely right about the power of nouns to evoke the world. The names of wild flowers, such as stitchwort, lady's bedstraw and feverfew, are one- or two-word poems that transport us instantly out of doors. The denaturing of the dictionary is part of the denaturing of our lives, not just a symptom of it. The writer Robert Macfarlane has called for a "rewilding" of the language, a revival of old, parochial words for nature as one way of shaking us out of our indoor, virtual existences. "The right names, well used, can act as portals," he writes. "Good names open on to mystery, grow knowledge and summon wonder." When we don't know the names of living things, we care about them less, and retreat a little from the real. Nouns should bring us closer to the world.

•

That all makes sense. But then—then you try to sort the concrete from the abstract nouns and find that it is not so easy. *Money* is reassuringly concrete when it is cotton paper notes or metal alloy coins, but ominously abstract when it is numbers dancing and leaping along a broker's computer screen. *Laughter* feels concrete when you hear it, this natural music that no other animal makes, an involuntary gasp of approval more precious and truth-telling than applause. But you can't see it or hold it, and every comedian wishes they could bottle it to stop it dying on the air without an echo. Modern technology such as microscopes and CAT scans renders things concrete that we cannot apprehend with our unaided senses. Were bedbugs and radio waves not real before we could see them?

We need concrete nouns to name solid things, and abstract nouns to give the vague notions in our heads a nouny solidity.

Only with both of them can we capture what it is like to be human and alive. Our home is the Earth, the rocky planet on which we are all stranded. Gravity traps us here; that and the absence of other livable Earths less than light years away. Our bodies trap us in our selves. We need to lug them around, these stubbornly actual things, to sate our basic needs for food, fluids, warmth and sleep.

But, as Merton saw, that same Earth is also full of people in mad pursuit of things with no concrete reality at all. "The 'world' is not just a physical space traversed by jet planes and full of people running in all directions," he wrote. "It is a complex of responsibilities and options made out of the loves, the hates, the fears, the joys, the hopes, the greed, the cruelty, the kindness, the faith, the trust, the suspicion of all." We are bodies made of meat, blood and bone, but also of love, worry and longing.

Life is both concrete and abstract—and the abstract can feel very concrete. Merton came to think that much of modern life was a lie we told each other, a shadow we chased after while ignoring the world around us. What we needed more than happiness was approval, and it was destroying our chance of happiness. We were all striving to be moons to someone else's sun, which just made us moons of one another, living in perpetual darkness. Our social masks had stuck to our faces and we no longer knew the difference between skin and prosthesis. "A weird life it is, indeed," he wrote, "to be living always in somebody else's imagination, as if that were the only place in which one could at last become real!" But this weird life, as Merton also saw, was also real. The things that live only in our heads are often the things we hold most dear. Abstractions matter, and a writer's job is to write about them, however hard it might be.

•

In the autumn of 1938, the linguist Sam Hayakawa devised a concept for his freshman class at the University of Wisconsin.

Alarmed by fascist propaganda, Hayakawa wanted to make his students aware of what happens when words unfasten themselves from observable reality. Language was the lifeblood of what he called the "huge cooperative nervous system" of society. For that nervous system to work well, language had to work well, too.

Imagine, Hayakawa said, all the nouns and noun phrases in the world on a ladder. On the bottom rung sit the most concrete nouns: *chairs*, *walls*, *hands*, *feet*. On the middle rungs perch those specific–general words that sit somewhere between the abstract and the concrete. These words are both real things and categories for things: *breakfast*, *cigarettes*, *leftovers*. They are concrete but cannot be counted or split into single units. Hence *clothing*, not *underpants*; *fruit*, not *bunch of grapes*; *stationery*, not *fountain pen*. On the top rung are the abstract nouns, although some of these, like *depression* or *cancer*, feel scarily real. *Ladder* is concrete if you mean the one with vertical poles and horizontal rungs that you use to clear out your gutters, but abstract if you mean the figurative one that Hayakawa gave to his whole concept: the "ladder of abstraction."

The ladder of abstraction is a blunt but useful tool. Most usefully, it clarifies that there is nothing wrong with abstract nouns. Certain words have a close relation to the immediate world we perceive with our senses; others rely on secondhand information. Unlike other animals, humans do not just use their own data collection to find stuff out; they use data collected by others. Abstractions are how people share this secondhand knowledge, coming up with broad categories for things that, for convenience's sake, ignore differences. The word *home* ignores the differences between houses, apartments, bungalows and that blurrily mapped place where the heart belongs. Without this abstracting quality, we could never share with strangers all the things we know.

No single noun fully describes anything. The more concrete a noun, the more people agree on its meaning. But being concrete limits a noun's use, too, by tethering it tight to one sense.

Climbing the ladder of abstraction makes a concrete thing more evocative, by linking it to broad notions we all have some idea about. Abstraction fogs meaning, but the fog can be welcoming. Everyone knows roughly what *love, joy* and *sorrow* are. Abstractions are vague, but inclusively so.

Writing stuck on one rung of the ladder of abstraction is too monotone. Arguments that use only abstract nouns, like *truth* and *power* and *knowledge*, are hard to care about because writing that sidesteps the senses is dull. Sentimental or pious writing also leans on abstractions, replacing difficult feelings with consoling simplifications. When words are too general, they paint inadequate pictures. But writing that describes only the feelable things in front of our faces is also dull, because it does not say why those things should matter to someone else. Writing stuck on the ladder's middle rungs is worst of all, because here sit words with an illusory concreteness. Keep shinning up and down the ladder, though, and the reader gets the gist in different ways. She grasps big ideas through concrete things, and concrete things through big ideas. The tangible ignites the elusive and both of them shine brighter.

•

We have a word for this work that words do, grounding the abstract in the real: metaphor. We tend to see metaphor as literary embroidery, what the poet Mark Doty calls "frosting on the cake of sense." But really it is just language in its natural state, especially when it is trying to gauge the unknown by setting it against the known. Metaphor is how we nail the jelly of reality to the wall. The Bible is full of vivid metaphors because it is trying to give form to the formless. That ultimate unknowable, God, is continually compared to something else: a father, a king, a shepherd, a farmer, a builder, a potter, a vintner, a tailor, a lion, an eagle, a leopard, a moth, a withering wind, and dry rot.

We also need metaphor to grasp things that are perfectly real but that boggle our minds. The deep time of geology, or the inhuman scale of astronomy, or the unknown alcoves of the brain, all need metaphor to get our heads round them because they defy the limits of human perspective and scramble understanding. So we shrink or supersize them to an earthly scale. The virtual world of the Internet we imagine as an actual world. *Websites* are places you visit. *Home pages* are familiar spaces you return to and the start of a book whose virtual leaves you can turn over by clicking on links. Even when data floats in a wireless nowhere, we liken its location to something ethereal but real: *the cloud.*

Metaphor describes the indescribable by relating it to the bare facts of our lives, which are these: We are two-legged animals who stand upright. Standing upright raises our heads, so we peer horizontally out at the world, through small holes in our skull, from an altitude of a few feet. It also frees up those non-locomotory limbs, arms, to touch, feel and grip. The bilateral symmetry of our bodies makes us see ourselves as the center of the world, facing ahead and looking around, with binocular vision and stereophonic sound. We live in our own bodies, see through our own eyes and stand on one piece of earth at a time.

Metaphor returns us to these truths. In metaphor we are always, just like our bodies, moving nearer to or further away from things. *This sentence I'm struggling with isn't quite there yet. Your words really touched me.* Gravity makes us connect *up* with *good*, and *down* with *bad*. We use concrete space to grab hold of abstract time. The meeting was four hours *long*. Christmas has *come round* again and we are only *in* November. We fit feelings like love inside bodily vessels like the heart—although wouldn't the stomach (delicate, wayward, unruly) be a more fitting holdall?

Scientists in human sentence-processing have shown that a dead metaphor—like *falling* in love or *surfing* the Web—sparks little brain activity in someone reading it. But a fresh metaphor briefly excites the brain. It is odd enough for readers to notice but plausible enough for them to accept its slight recalibration of the world. It is at once a discovery and a rediscovery, a place where surprise and recognition meet. The philosopher Max Black wrote that metaphor does not so much compare something to something else as alter what both those things mean. Calling a man a wolf renders him more like a wolf, but it also renders the wolf more like a man. A fresh metaphor acts on both tenor and vehicle. It aims to make the strange familiar and ends up making the familiar strange.

No metaphor is disinterested. It says how it feels about something without overliteralizing or belaboring the point. A metaphor's potency comes from its being so hard to refute. It lodges in the reader's mind without the writer having to explain and defend it. A simile is a thought-out affinity; a metaphor is meaning in shorthand. Metaphors are seductive because they seem to open up, in William Empson's words, a "loophole for common sense." They are descriptions that are also, invisibly, arguments.

The model Kate Moss, once asked for her motto, replied: "Nothing tastes as good as skinny feels." A dubious message to send about body image, perhaps, but a well-turned sentence, surely—which is why it is so well known. The metaphor arrives with the word *skinny*, usually an adjective but here turned into an abstract noun, paired with another abstract noun, *nothing*. But *skinny* is also concrete, because where it lies in the sentence suggests that it can actually be felt, just as food has a taste. The clincher is that *feels* also retains some trace of the other, non-sensual sense of experiencing or intuiting something (*skinny feels good*). As the sentence ends with the snap of a stressed syllable, one's slant has been altered in a way that feels true. The world has shifted on its axis, then clicked back into place, because *nothing tastes as good as skinny feels*.

•

Abstract nouns are not the enemy of good writing. What matters is what kind of abstract nouns they are and how they shift the balance of the writing. Writing drifts into obscurity when it overuses a certain kind of abstract noun: a nominalization. A nominalization makes a verb (or sometimes an adjective) into a noun. It turns *act* into *action*, *react* into *reaction*, *interact* into *interaction*. It gives a process a name.

According to the linguist Michael Halliday, the nominalization emerged in the seventeenth century, with the birth of modern science. To describe what they were doing, these pioneer scientists needed a way of turning single events into general laws. Before then, to explain nature's workings, or to write up experiments, they had to use a full clause, with a subject and a verb. *The apple fell from the tree* because *this small spherical object was drawn to a much bigger one, the Earth*. Nominalizations let them hide clauses, which describe an event, inside a noun, which gave that event a name. The apple's *descent* was a *result* of *gravitation*.

A nominalization implies that a process has stayed still long enough for us to name it. It turns a live event into a sedentary thing. Scientific language sees the world like this, as a series of things to be identified and classified. It breaks up nature's ceaseless flow into inert parts, as if it were dismantling a clock and laying out its cogs, gears, weights and springs neatly for inspection.

Nominalizations pack a lot into single words. Science needs them so it does not waste time going over old news. It is quicker to say that a hummingbird's hum is made by its *rapid wingbeats* (a nominalizing noun phrase) than by its *beating its wings rapidly*. But if you bury too many verbs under nouns, you shut out the layperson, for whom the stuff that is old to an expert is new. And even experts find sentences chockful of nouns uninviting—even when they know what the nouns mean. Brevity has been bought at the cost of clarity and ease.

A nominalization traps energy inside it, turning fluid actions into unmoving things. It is the white dwarf of the sentence. A white dwarf is the shrunken remains of a star, in which gravity has packed the protons and electrons so tight that a spoonful of matter weighs tons. A nominalization is the shrunken remains of a verbal clause, a noun-heavy mass compacted with pre-learned knowledge. But pre-learned by whom? Your reader, you hope—but you can't be sure.

•

The nominalization arose in math and the physical sciences of physics, chemistry and astronomy. In these fields there is no life or death, just the inanimate universe of numbers, energy and matter. In Newtonian law, the cosmos runs like clockwork. Nothing truly new or random occurs, even if the cosmic deck-chairs are rearranged occasionally. The universe has no intention or emotion. Shit happens. To explain such a place, nominalizations, like *friction, repulsion* and *acceleration*, are ideal.

As science gained cachet, though, the nominalization spread elsewhere. In the nineteenth century it conquered the more fluid science of biology. And in the twentieth century it conquered the social sciences, government and business as a way of describing how society works. But society is made up of people, and people do not behave predictably, like stars, rocks or other animals. We are contrarians, full of capricious energies and self-defeating desires. We are mysteries to each other and mysterious even to ourselves. We act like verbs, not nouns.

In these worlds the nominalization is often ritualistic, there to coat writing with a pseudo-objective finish. Such writing is full of abstract nouns with endings like *-ity, -ism, -ology* and *-ation*. Sometimes big nouns are born of perfectly good smaller nouns. *Transport* begets *transportation, time* begets *temporality, position* begets *positionality*. Often nouns pair up with meta-nouns, words not so much for things as for the categories into which they fit, like *notion, issue* or *level*. A common piece of sentence flab includes both noun or adjective and category: period of *time*, circular in *shape*, weather *conditions*. Single nouns grow into noun strings, in which the nouns retool as pseudo-adjectives. In theory these strings, like *supply chain resource issues* or *website content delivery platform*, turn all but the last noun into an adjective. In practice, we read them all as nouns until we get to the last one and have to untie the whole string.

In the 1970s the poet Elizabeth Bishop taught writing seminars at Harvard. Shy and nervous leading classes, she still managed to produce a long, confident list for her students headed "If you want to write well avoid these words." Many of the words were nominalizations, like *creativity*, *sensitivity* and "most ivity-words." Others were those dressed-up noun categories that have crept into daily use and distance us from the real: *life-experience*, *relationship*, *aspect*, *area*, *potential*, *structure*, *lifestyle*. *Lifestyle*, which back then was hyphenated or written as two words, was also censured by Christopher Lasch in a style guide he wrote for his students at the University of Rochester in 1985. "The appeal of this tired but now ubiquitous phrase probably lies in its suggestion that life is largely a matter of style," he wrote. "Find something else to say about life."

English is getting nounier. More than half the words in the dictionary are nouns and the number rises each year. Linguists work with a huge sample of language called a *corpus*, with which they track how words are used. These corpora were once harvested onerously by hand. Now it is all done electronically, creating vast databanks of sentences. Whole libraries of books can be quickly scanned—even without opening them, using terahertz waves that percolate the pages and their chiaroscuro of ink and blank space so the words can be deciphered by an optical character reader. With such modern magic we mine the billions of ways, over hundreds of years, that writers have woven words into sentences. This is how we know that English is filling up with nouns.

The American writer and educator John Erskine once wrote

that "the noun is only a grappling iron to hitch your mind to the reader's." If the reader does not know roughly what it refers to already, the sentence in which it appears may be a short unmeeting of minds. On the other hand, turning something into a noun makes it tangible. Words like *reification* or *governance* become hardy things that, to the initiated, speak for themselves. A noun may try to convince the reader that something is real, and may even succeed. *Website content delivery platform* is not just a noun, but four nouns—so it *must* be a thing. It lives!

Merton thought that the same thing happened to big religious nouns like *mercy* or *contemplation*. They took on a nouny reality and came to be incanted for inspirational or magical effect. Before long their nouniness began to seem like "an objective quality, a spiritual commodity that one can procure ... something which, when possessed, liberates one from problems and from unhappiness."

Noun-speak bears the traces of that tribal faith in word magic, the belief that chanting words like a spell brings something into being, whether it be a cattle plague for one's enemy or a good harvest for oneself. We flatter ourselves, us modern skeptics, that we are rational and unillusioned and have left such primitive notions behind. But word magic survives in curses, oaths—and nouns.

•

For Merton, the noun-stuffed sentence was a canker on modern prose. In one of his last essays, "War and the Crisis of Language," written in 1968 as America mired itself in Vietnam, he showed how this cankerous writing amputated us from reality. He began with an odd analogy: the revival among evangelical Christians of glossolalia, or speaking in tongues. The speaker in tongues, who is meant to be channeling the Holy Spirit, is actually talking fluent gibberish. To speak in tongues is to speak without fear of dissent. You cannot be gainsaid because no one knows what you are saying, least of all you.

Merton saw glossolalia as a metaphor for much modern writing, which is "locked tight upon itself, impenetrable, unbreakable, irrefutable." Dwelling in a closed circuit of unmeaning, this writing permits no reply. It has moved so far from the verbal energy of speech that it has lost all sense of a voice speaking to an audience. It has been written by no one to be read by no one. It is anti-language, a weary run-through of the linguistic motions.

Merton went on to examine American government statements about Vietnam, with their hypnotically bland vocabulary of *pacification*, *escalation* and *liberation*. The words felt chlorine-washed of life. But beneath the flat nouns and lumbering syntax lay horrible truths. *Enemy structures* were the burned huts of razed villages. *Vietcong* were the charred bodies of the villagers. The *kill ratio* was how many more of those bodies there were than those of American soldiers.

Around this time Merton was also thinking about Adolf Eichmann. The most troubling aspect of the Eichmann trial for him was that a psychiatrist examined the defendant and found him quite sane. He felt no guilt, ate heartily and slept well. He spoke and wrote in a desiccated official language with which he seemed to have convinced himself of his own sweet reasonableness.

The Eichmann trial had taken place in Jerusalem in the spring and summer of 1961. Over a hundred Holocaust survivors came one by one to the witness box. Each gave devastating testimony: of being forced into ghettos, confined in cattle trucks, marched through dark forests in the frozen winter and then set to work as slave labor in the camps, having to live with the constant smell of death as their fellow prisoners were shot and gassed around them. In the dock, behind glass, sat Eichmann. All the evidence pointed to his having overseen the deportations, signed death warrants and visited the camps to see his orders being met.

Eichmann was now in his mid fifties, thickly bespectacled, his hairline receding, his voice deep and calm. He had the air of a slightly overextended middle manager. When cross-examined, he answered in one-note monologues. Asked about forcing Jews to wear the Yellow Star, he would go off on a long detour about police regulations for official letters, the protocol for getting the department chief's signature and the meaning of all the different colors of ink. As the prosecutors got ever more irritated, he sounded ever more dignified and dull.

And how did this company man defend himself? With an impenetrable shield of nouns. He described his role as "emigration specialist." The Auschwitz death trains were "evacuation transport." Things either fell, or more likely did not fall, within his "area of competence." Where he could, he hid behind the passive voice. "Everything was geared to the idea of emigration," he said. "But constant difficulties were caused by various offices in a bureaucratic manner." Of the Wannsee Conference, which finalized plans for murdering all the Jews in German-occupied Europe, he said only that "the various types of possible solutions were discussed." He spoke in the stock phrases that were how he had come to think and see. As Hannah Arendt wrote in the *New Yorker*, "Eichmann's mind was filled to the brim with such sentences."

•

This noun-ridden language—stale, self-proving, sleepwalking from one big noun to the next—has become the argot of modern managerialism. To measure its staleness, count the nouns. The nouniness of a piece of writing is a sure sign of lack of care for the reader and lack of thought in the writer. For writing is not just a way of communicating; it is a way of thinking. Nouny writing relieves the writer of the need to do either.

In nouny writing, anything can be claimed and nothing can be felt. No one says who did what to whom, or takes ownership or blame. Instead of saying that *x is not working* (verb and participle), they say that there has been a *loss of functionality* (two nouns) *in x*. These words are not even trying to illuminate; they are immunizing themselves against the world. The aim, even if unknown to the writer, is to bore the reader into not looking closely at the words. Instead of inviting a response, as writing should, it shuts it down.

Nouny sentences are the Sargasso Sea of prose. The actual Sargasso Sea is bound within a circular system of currents called the North Atlantic Gyre. These currents turn the sea into a garbage patch, as the congealed oil, plastic and other debris carried into it has no way out. In the days when ships needed sails, they could be stranded here for weeks waiting for a gust of wind. The sea is almost a marine desert, the surface waters taking so long to change that they are depleted of nutrients. All that grows there is the floating sargassum seaweed after which it is named. Sargasso Sea prose is like this: flat, becalmed, full of the tar balls, junk and seaweed of inert nouns, and stuck in its own little microclimate, away from the swirling, tidal ocean of life.

When people try to hide their personalities behind procedures, they enter this Sargasso Sea of sentences. When they want to sound rational and reasonable, but to avoid mentioning any inconveniently actual people—living, thinking, suffering, struggling to survive just like them—they use words voided of meaning, like *modernization* or *incentivization*. No one has to teach them to write this way, just as no one has to teach a grown-up eel, swimming happily in a European or American river, to turn tail and find its way thousands of miles back to the real Sargasso Sea, where it will mate, spawn and die. An eel knows when and where to go; a writer knows when and where to start writing nounily. The switch in the brain has been flicked.

Mostly this kind of uncommunication is tedious but harmless. But Merton saw that, because it sounds so boringly sane, it could make the insane sound routine—even the insanity of napalm death, nuclear war or genocide. Inside such artificially sealed-off language, the maddest realities seem sensible. When nouns rule over sentences, all the air has been punched out of them. Emptied of life and humanity, they have been refilled with inertia and nothingness. All the imaginative promise of words has been pulped into a lumpy noun gravy, neither liquid enough to flow nor solid enough to be forked. This noun gravy is tasteless but, should we swallow enough of it, noxious.

•

The best thing that happened to Merton as a writer was that Gethsemani turned out not to be quite the deliverance he had first thought. After the ecstasy of his arrival, he began to feel weighed down by work and to suffer from insomnia and depression. In this world of almost silence, he became neurotically sensitive to the noise of the farm machines and the monks clomping around in their metal-shod boots or snoring loudly in the dorm. He still had joyous moments, but now wrestled with the usual unsaintly umbrages. As his mood worsened, his writing improved. He came to regret the tone of his early writings, with their florid piety and virtuous scorn toward the world and its profane inhabitants. A writer, he decided, should be true to human conflictedness, open to all our absurdities and incongruities.

This was Merton's great gift as a writer. He was a religious thinker whose subject was not the next world but this one, not the pure light of the afterlife but the murky light of this life. He lost patience with the monastic ideal of *contemptus mundi*, which saw the world as sad, sinful and to be fled as soon as possible. He grew to hate those pictures used to illustrate magazine features about Trappists, of the cowl-covered monk with his back to the camera, staring at a lake. Being alive meant being open to the world, he felt, not hiding behind esoteric observances.

By the mid 1960s Merton was living full-time in his hut, feeling a new kinship with the bachelor farmers who worked alone in the Kentucky hills. The only human sound he could hear now was the occasional shake of his windows as guns went off at Fort Knox. But even as he became a hermit, he thought of the Christian mission as choosing to be part of humanity. He weighed his newfound solitude against the loneliness he had once felt. Loneliness was pointless and depleting; solitude reacquainted you more lastingly with life. He now saw himself as a "guilty bystander," full of anger about the unfairnesses of the world.

The aliveness of Merton's writing, its winning blend of the abstract and concrete, of vivid nouns and strong verbs, came from his living in this no man's land between holiness and humanity. From his hut he would see jet planes passing far above Kentucky and imagine the business executives inside, all dressed in washable suits, drinking vodka martinis and spooning down airline meals, in a high-speed living room that had risen from the earth in Florida to land again in Illinois. A world like this, he decided—weird enough to bring him into such unlikely contact with these fellow mortals calmly defying gravity—was a worthy subject for a writer, even a religious one.

Merton thought that writing should be true to our self-quarreling natures. Like the quality of mercy, it should free us from the insane compulsion to be consistent. The writer's task was not to cut some hard diamond of unanswerable truth, but to allow communication to occur. Sentences need some give in them. They must be open to dispute by a truth the writer does not own and the reader might see differently. They must bring us back to the human realm of fine distinctions and honest doubts. Reality is not there to be hunted and speared with sentences. In good writing, problems are lived, not solved—are held and weighed with words, not beaten with a stick until they are tamed.

•

How do you breathe life into sentences choked with nouns? Simple: use verbs. Disinter the buried verbs and bring them back to life by reverbing them. Unspool the noun strings, restoring the proper links between the nouns by adding verbs and prepositions, even if this means using more words. Turn weak verb–noun phrases into verbs. *Puts emphasis on: emphasizes. Gives the impression: suggests. Draws attention to: notes.* Turn other parts of speech into verbs. Verbs born of adjectives—we *dim* lights, *tame* hair, *muddy* prose—can be especially cinematic.

I say all this is simple, but tying noun phrases together with weak verbal knots is simple. Adding strong verbs is hard. A sentence should be a labor to write, not to read. Nouny sentences are the reverse: a labor to read, a breeze to write. Those who write them assume that, just by gumming nouns together, they have communicated with other human beings. All they have achieved is a lazy, bogus fluency.

Only about a seventh of the words in the dictionary are verbs. In polls of favorite words, verbs barely figure. The popular words are nouns, especially (despite the censure they receive in the style books) long abstract nouns like *serendipity* or *mellifluousness*, and long adjectives like *effervescent* or *sempiternal*. But these big words always disappoint. They sound luminescent (another high-polling word) on their own, but in sentences they burn too brightly and suck the life out of words around them, like stars that have turned into black holes.

People who love words—crossword solvers, anagram lovers, Scrabble players—love nouns and adjectives. But people who love sentences love verbs. Nouns, because they name something permanent, have just one form. Of all parts of speech they are the most self-sufficient and singularly resonant. But verbs take many forms, often irregular, depending on what role they play in the sentence. They are useless by themselves, and rarely as euphonious as nouns or adjectives. But put them next to other words and they are as life-giving to the sentence as light and air are to the world.

Verbs enact this universal law: everything moves. The Earth orbits around a sun, tilting and swiveling as it goes, speeding a hundred miles through space in the five seconds you took to read this sentence. As the Earth tilts and swivels, the share of sunlight each part of it receives changes, and the seasons change with it, a cycle of springing to life and dying back. That gaseous veneer coating the Earth, atmosphere, combines with the sun's heat and the Earth's spin to make weather. Weather gives each day a different-flavored soup of wind, heat and rain. In just the right amounts this soup allows for life.

Life is movement. Each day we take 23,000 breaths and our hearts beat 100,000 times. These breathing lungs and beating hearts allow us to move around and make our way in the world. Life needs energy to sustain it and energy burns itself out. And so our lives burn themselves out in the end and we return to the topsoil from which all life comes. Life begins again.

Modern science, which needed the nominalization to invent itself, has come round to this idea of reality as permanent flux. The Swiss-watch precision of the Newtonian world order is no more. Scientific laws still hold, but now we know that complex systems are so sensitive to initial conditions that chaos ensues. A moth flapping its wings in Catford can cause a tornado in Caracas. In quantum theory, all particles in the universe are in disequilibrium, a never-ending becoming. Even inside rock-solid objects, subatomic particles scud around at unearthly speeds. Solid things only seem solid because their movements are too small to be seen. Things are not things but happenings. Nothing stays still, ever. *Life* is a noun but it can only be lived as a verb.

Merton, though no scientist, got all this. Looking out at the world from his hut's wooden porch, he became a zealous convert to its endless ongoingness, its verbiness. Many of his journal entries now simply recorded the changing evidence of his senses. He noted the fireflies flitting, the crickets and cicadas clicking, the catbirds and bobwhites bickering, and the loblolly pines and red maples shaking in the wind. He felt as if he had unearthed nature's open secret, there for all to see if we just looked: every single moment makes itself anew.

The Catholic Merton now embraced Taoism and Zen. These Buddhist faiths see every living thing as like a sunrise or sunset, its beauty at one with its brevity, all things arising and then passing away. A Buddhist life is lived in the fluid now, without cleaving to some unattainable dream of the past or future. Eastern mysticism and modern science agree: reality is unbroken flow. Nouns divide that flow into things. They press the pause button of language and freeze-frame the real. Verbs set it in motion again.

•

Some verbs, though, have more life in them than others. The most common verb is *to be*, deployed in roughly half of all English sentences. "I am," wrote John Clare, "yet what I am none cares or knows." Hard to imagine a sentence more alive than that: what could be more vital than affirming one's being to an indifferent world? But *I am* more often forms a copula, a linking verb. It says that the subject is the same thing as something else (*I am a smoker*) or has the same quality as something else (*I am smoking*). When you use *to be* like this, to say that something is something else, the verb has less life—the least possible life, in fact, for it merely states the bare fact of existence.

In a 1965 essay, "To Be or Not to Be," an American linguist, David Bourland, proposed a new language called E-Prime, which stripped English of *to be*. This verb was, he felt, a shortcut for the mind—the word equivalent of an equal sign. It propped up a whole tradition in Western logic, back to Aristotle, which ascribed fixed identities to things. In fact, Bourland wrote, nothing really equates to anything else. The essence of life is change. *To be* foists a fake permanence on the world. In the mere second we use to say that this rose is red, it has transformed into a slightly different rose, and *red* is an elastic quality anyway, only grasped by comparing its shade and hue to something else, like blood or lipstick.

Bourland took his lead from ecology, a verb-loving science which sees the world as a perpetual balancing act of codependent parts. E-Prime, he felt, might help to eliminate the empty tautologies of politicians, which imply that the past and present have one meaning and the future one course. Therapists might use it to help us escape those absolutist statements that make us so miserable. Instead of seeing myself as a static noun (*I'm an idiot*) or adjective (*I'm so idiotic*), I can use a dynamic verb (*I behaved like an idiot*). The most wretchedly rigid-seeming realities can be lived down.

Bourland also disliked *to be* because it went with the passive voice. The passive turns the object of an actively voiced clause (I spilled *the pint of beer*) into the subject (*The pint of beer* was spilled by me). Style guides frown on it because it departs from the active rhythms of speech and weakens the force of the words. Concerns *were expressed*. We are sorry for *any inconvenience caused*. The passive lets people present their euphemistic stone-walling as if it were stubborn truth.

The passive thwarts our healthy desire to ascribe acts to actors and give events a sense of verbal drive. A neat way to meet this desire is to use the mediopassive instead. The mediopassive looks like an active clause, but the subject is really the object, so it shows an action without an actor. *This sentence reads well.* English can use the mediopassive because it does not need to mark an active agent—unlike, say, French, which needs a reflexive pronoun. The mediopassive has grown in use over the past century, especially in ad copy, because it brings inert things to life. *This butter melts on the tongue. This car handles like a dream.*

And yet our style-guide censure of the passive voice is only about a hundred years old. Skilled writers ignore it. They use the passive sparingly but inventively, to stagger the release of information in a sentence. They say *The experiment was conducted* because English has no easy way of referring to a non-specific executor of an action. (*We* sometimes works, but it presumes that we agree who *we* is.) They say *My iPhone was stolen*, not just because they do not know who stole it, but because the point is that they no longer have an iPhone. They say *The shells are discarded by hermit crabs* because that sentence is not *Hermit crabs discard the shells* written differently. One is about the shells; the other is about the hermit crabs.

The passive can bring the real point of the sentence into view. Perhaps there is too much to say about the subject for it all to be slotted in before the verb. So shift the subject to the end of the sentence as the object, and it spreads out across the wide-open space beyond the main verb. Now it will be easier to unpack once the rest of the sentence has been read. The Angel of the North was stolen by *art thieves who cut its ankles with an angle grinder, lugged it on to the back of a lorry and made their getaway on the A1.* Here the art thieves and their modus operandi draw more attention than Antony Gormley's artwork. The long phrase at the end of the sentence bears most of the weight.

The passive may be less vigorous than the active, but it may also be more truthful. A sentence should feel alive, but not stupidly hyperactive. We live a lot in the passive voice, since reality is an authorless poem being written without our help. Cushioned by the bubble wrap of modern comforts, we convince ourselves that we decide our fates. But we are just carbon-based life forms, careering through space on a medium-sized planet. We were thrown into the world without being consulted, and will be thrown out of it when a major organ gives up on us. Our bodies are husks, carrier bags for our genes, which are our only shot at immortality. That gelatinous hunk of protein that is sussing out these sentences, your brain, will one day remind you that you are not its master. Sometimes life just *is*.

•

Bourland failed to persuade us all to abandon *to be*. People still say *Roses are red* and not *I see this rose as red* or *This rose seems red to me*. E-Prime never caught on because it is too hard to do well. Novices resort to a pidgin E-Prime that swaps *seems* or *appears* for *is* and ends up sounding tentative. Or they overuse *to have*—*the sausages have cooked*—which sees the world in terms of stable qualities and possessions. A world without *to be* would not be a utopia of open-minded mutability. We cannot so easily rid ourselves of fixed ideas and stale notions; we just find new ways to be fixed and stale.

Without *to be*, it is harder to imagine that without which there is no hope: the future. You can use the simple present to say *We leave for Tahiti next week*. But you can't say *We are to be wed on the beach and will be wearing flower garlands and toasting ourselves with mojitos*. Without *to be* we also lose a lot of metaphor. Gone would be most of Ian Hamilton Finlay's luminous aphorisms, like *Illness is a sort of exile from the everyday* or *Honey was the gasoline of antiquity*.

A *to be* sentence can sound plain but still pack in a quiet profundity. "I begin," writes Wendell Berry at the start of one essay, "with the proposition that eating is an agricultural act." He means that because we all eat, we are all answerable for the health of the food chain. If that goes awry, we share the liability with everyone else in the chain. Hooked on cheap food, we ignore its hidden costs—the poisoning of fields with pesticides, the cruelty to livestock, the loss of small farms, the joylessly fuel-driven mode of eating all this enables—and pass on the blame. We come to see ourselves as islanded from the land.

That *is* in Berry's sentence asks us to think of the dinner plate as food's final stop on a long journey. It wants us to see that handing over money for shrink-wrapped meat, pre-chopped veggies and pillow packs of wilting salad is ... odd. What does it actually mean, he asks, to subcontract our hunter-gathering to supermarkets, which sell us sweet and salty approximations of real food that only leave us wanting more?

To be sentences help us to notice these links that habit has made invisible. Berry's simple statement—"Eating [*subject*] is [*verb*] an agricultural act [*complement*]"—invites us to think hard about how we live. At its heart is the idea that farming is about balance, and that failure to preserve that balance is a kind of sickness. If we do not take care of all the things we use, even if we only got them by proxy, we are living the wrong life.

Today's drug of choice is convenience. We live cut off from its side effects, surrounded by unnoticed magic. We flick a switch and light or heat decants from the expected places. We grab a pint of milk from a supermarket shelf, tap our contactless card at the automated checkout and walk out of the shop without a word. We stroke the glass screen nestled in our palm and watch it rustle up, twenty minutes later, a deliveryman with a thermal bag strapped to his back like a tortoiseshell, out of which he whips a flat box containing a disc of baked, blistered dough with chewy cheese on top. Just to describe such a world is to reveal its strangeness. *To be* helps us to notice it anew.

To be works best for crisp observations and assertions that make us see things afresh. Check all the times you use *is* and *was* in your writing and see if they are just linking things weakly or actually saying something worth saying. A *to be* sentence can be mind-altering. This is the way the world is, it says: hadn't you noticed?

•

Now that we know what *to be* is for, we can concede that Bourland had a point. Writing infected with too much *to be* is indeed soggy and flat. Bourland devised a useful "crispness index," to measure the ratio of E-Prime sentences in classic texts, in which Aristotle scored lowest and Hemingway highest. He found poems by Blake, Shelley, Keats and Yeats all written in perfect E-Prime, for poetry loves strong verbs.

An adjective and preposition added to *is* means wasted words, ones that can be saved with stronger verbs. *Is applicable to: applies to. Is indicative of: indicates. Is able to: can. To be* goes with nouny writing. When you bury a verb in a nominalization, a weak verb like *to be* often follows it. An action with a strong verb (*Rutherford split the atom)* becomes a static noun phrase (*Rutherford's splitting of the atom*), which then needs a weak verb like *was,* or maybe *led to* or *resulted in,* to solder it to the rest of the sentence.

Too much *to be* makes for wordy set-ups like *what is crucial here is.* These can sometimes give the reader a helpful running jump before the real subject arrives. But academic writing hides too often behind them. *This is reflective of. It could be said to. It is evident from the data that.* Nervous public speakers clear their throats before they start speaking, something every actor or singer knows not to do because it just inflames the vocal cords. *There are* and *it is* are a sort of textual throat-clearing that succeeds only in blocking the airways more. When joined to a relative pronoun like *who* or *that,* they can always be cut. *There are three poets who have given drunken readings at our college. Three poets have given drunken readings at our college.* Some writers, in an effort to paper over the problem with informality, turn *it is* into *it's.* The only cure is to use *it is* less.

•

The American art historian Ernest Fenollosa, in his classic essay "The Chinese Written Character as a Medium for Poetry" (*c.*1903), claimed that the truest poetry, indeed the truest language, avoids *to be.* It uses only the transitive verb—an action verb with a direct object. Even copulas have their origins in actions. *Is* comes from the Aryan root *as,* "to breathe," *be* from the Indo-European *bhu,* "to become," and *was* from the Sanskrit *vas,* "to stay." For Fenollosa, when we use a copula merely to link one bit of a sentence to another we deny the dynamic reality of all verbs and of life itself.

Fenollosa wrote of "the tyranny of medieval logic," which saw thought as "a kind of brickyard." In this brickyard, ideas were baked into bricks and labeled with words. Writing a sentence meant picking out bricks and building a wall, with white mortar for *is* and black mortar for *is not*. With such a word wall you can write a sentence like *A ring-tailed baboon is not a constitutional assembly*. But all you are doing is arresting the real at a point where you can say what it is, or isn't. Fenollosa credits Shakespeare with shaking us out of this medieval fixation with *is* and teaching us instead to draw on English's rich hoard of transitive verbs, which treat nature as "a vast storehouse of forces."

Fenollosa is right about Shakespeare's verbiness. He is always turning nouns and adjectives into verbs: "uncle me no uncle," "gentle his condition." His compound adjectives capture little verbal choreographies: "heaven-kissing hill," "earth-treading stars," "lazy-pacing clouds," "fen-sucked fogs." And, as the linguist Jonathan Hope notes, he loves to bring the inert to life. In the phrase "proud hoofs i' th' receiving earth," the adjectives confer verbal animacy on the dead tissue of a horse's hoofs and the insensate earth—which is not just imprinted with the hoofs, but *receives* them. Even when he uses other parts of speech, Shakespeare is all about the verbs.

For Fenollosa, neither "a true noun, an isolated thing," nor "a pure verb, an abstract motion," occurs in nature. Nature is things meeting up with actions. The Chinese ideogram is both poetic and truthful because it combines noun and verb, painting and music, into one. In ideograms, even abstract nouns are concrete, because the words are also pictures. *Spring*: the sun rising over green shoots. *East:* the sun snagged in a tree's branches. *Revenge*: hatred coated in snow. *Listening*: an ear, eye and heart, and a line tracing undivided attention.

Over 2,000 years ago, in the Qin dynasty, the Emperors' chancellor Li Si streamlined Chinese grammar. As only an autocrat can, he rid it of tenses, persons, moods, articles and irregular verbs. Each Chinese character was now a one-syllable word and you just had to put the words in the right order: subject, verb, object. The sentence *Man sees horse* is three ideograms. First, the subject: a man with two legs. Second, the verb: his eye moving through space, depicted as an eye with running legs underneath it. Third, the object: the horse with its four legs. Chinese likes to turn abstract notions into concrete pictures. It is full of proverbs that wrap our vague wishes in little stories. *Do not wish to be rare like jade, or common like stone. Read ten thousand books and walk ten thousand miles. A single thread cannot make a cord, nor a single tree a forest. A cunning rabbit has three warrens.*

For Fenollosa the most truthful form of words was a sentence made up of subject, verb and object. This classic syntax was forced upon our ancestors by the workings of the world. It mirrored the natural way that animate things did things to less animate things. In nature, force moves from an agent to an object. A flash of lightning is an electrical discharge from a cloud to the earth. Light is radiation moving from one place to another at the fastest speed in the universe. Heat is kinetic energy moving from one body to another, atom by atom. Gravity is a force of attraction between objects of different mass. Human will is transitive, too, acting on the world in some way—even if, as so often with humans, the change turns out to be perverse or self-defeating.

And yet, whatever Fenollosa says, we cannot get by with just transitive verbs. Verbs deal not only in actions like lightning flashes, but in moods, feelings and intuitions. In her book *Artful Sentences*, Virginia Tufte argues that different kinds of verbs have different levels of heat. By switching between them we dial the heat up and down, as if adjusting a thermostat. Transitive verbs have the most heat because the verb acts on an object. *We lit a fire*. A notch down the dial come the intransitive verbs, which do not need an object to act on. *We met. I sneezed. He flinched.* Linking verbs like *look*, *feel* and *seem* have even less heat. *To be* is the coldest of all.

Sometimes you need to warm a sentence up, sometimes cool it down. Copulas are cooling and calming. *It was mid-autumn and the leaves were on the turn*. But too many low-heat verbs freeze up the prose. Transitives dial the heat up again. A *to be* clause like *The young man was drinking some milk* has turned the drinking into an inert operation. But *The young man padded barefoot toward the fridge, took out a pint of milk, sniffed it gingerly, grunted approval and then slugged it straight from the bottle* relays an action that takes about as long as the reader needs to read about it. Skilled writing moves from action to stasis and back, easing the pace then ramping it up again. It joins the stability of identity, which gives us a fix on the world, with the heat of action, which makes it move.

•

A complete sentence needs at least one finite verb. A finite verb must agree with a subject and have a tense. *My brain hurts*. Like other finite things, a finite verb has limits. The limits are time (my brain is hurting now, but hopefully not forever) and the subject to which it is linked (my brain hurts, no one else's).

Non-finite verbs—infinitives (the basic form of a verb, usually beginning *to*), participles (verbal adjectives) and gerunds (verbal nouns)—do not need a tense or need to agree with a subject. Without a subject and tense, they have lost some of the heat of finite verbs. They can also create confusion about who is doing what to whom and when—hence that common problem, the dangling participle, which comes at the start of a sentence but forgets to refer to the subject. *Strolling* along London Bridge, *the Shard* loomed above us. Another problem is that both present participles and gerunds end in *-ing*. If you use lots of *-ing* words, it may be unclear if they are participles or gerunds or some other word ending in *-ing*. The result is samey-sounding *-ings* and temporal confusion.

But the temporal ambiguity of non-finite verbs is also an asset. They can float more freely in the sentence, adding verbal heat without the writer having to add a whole new clause. An infinitive phrase extends a sentence easily and retains much of the heat of a finite verb. She kept telling me *to take my finger out of my nose* so I learned *to pick it surreptitiously*. Even a gerund, which acts like a noun, has a little crackle of verbal life behind its nouny stillness. My *nose-picking* was my *undoing*.

Participles act like adjectives. The present participle has the most verbal heat. I was *looking* out of the plane's window and I saw the wing *burning*. The past participle has the least verbal heat because, with the verb *to be*, it forms the passive. The toast was *burned* and breakfast was *ruined*. But it can be used on its own, without the whole passive clause, to tighten the sentence. *The toast burned and breakfast ruined, we left the house hungry.*

A participial phrase can be sneaked in almost anywhere in a sentence to add an espresso shot of verbal verve. That horse *trotting up to the fence* is *angling for a sugar lump*. It can stretch out the sentence by adding a coda to the main clause. There I was, *stuck on an empty train platform as hope seeped away.* When two things happen at once, a main clause and participial phrase bring them neatly together. Please do not drool over my enormous milkshake, *panting like a lovesick puppy.* One of the habits of good writing is adding these non-finite phrases to main clauses to give them an extra lease of verbal life.

•

Verbs do not just put events in the past, present or future (tense); they say whether they are complete or ongoing (aspect). English has just two aspects: the continuous and the perfect. The continuous means that something is still happening. *We are having a sword fight*. The perfect means that it is all in the past. *We have had a sword fight*. But putting tense and aspect together can weave any pattern in the fabric of time, from the present perfect continuous (*We have been having a sword fight*) to the past perfect continuous (*We had been having a sword fight*).

The past perfect (or pluperfect), a mix of tense and aspect, refers to something that occurred further into the past than some other, aforementioned past. As the past tense of the past tense, it declares something to be truly over and done with. Shifting between it and the simple past lets the writer move along the arrow of time with great control. V. S. Naipaul's use of the past perfect in *A House for Mr. Biswas* suggests sober sagacity: "Worse, to have lived without even attempting to lay claim to one's portion of the earth; to have lived and died as one had been born, unnecessary and unaccommodated." Overdone, though, the past perfect fills a sentence with colorless *hads* and *wases* and enervates the action across long stretches of time. The simple past tense is less precise but avoids these awkward segues between the past and the even more past. Just as rationing *is* makes prose crisper, so does rationing *had*.

English has lots of tenses but, apart from the simple present and past, it needs auxiliary verbs to make them. Auxiliary verbs are the little words—*do, have, will*—that fine-tune other verbs. They add depth and shade but have the same drawbacks as *to be*, giving off low heat and stuffing sentences with repetitions. Auxiliaries accompany mealy-mouthed admissions and soft-soaping safety-speak. We *do* apologize for the late running of this service. In the unlikely event of a water landing, your seat cushion *may* be used as a flotation device.

A subset of the auxiliary is the modal verb, such as *might, could* and *shall*. Put beside stronger verbs, modals let you speculate on whether something is possible, certain or even real. Academic writing, which is all about sifting fine distinctions, is thick with modal verbs. Too many modal verbs hold up the writing with noncommittal *mights* and *coulds*. It is as if you are tiptoeing through your sentences, trying not to wake the pedant on your shoulder, who will bite your head off if you say something bold.

But sounding irresolute may also be the price we pay for honest uncertainty. Life is modal. Sometimes it helps to think of the world as slightly blurred. Therapists use modal verbs to get their patients to come up with better stories for their lives. The grieving, for instance, can find it hard to assign the simple past tense to the person they have lost. Modal verbs help them to see the dead as in some way living on. *She would have enjoyed this, had she been around.*

•

Had not a hand injury put an end to his brief career, the sociologist Richard Sennett might have been a cellist. A child prodigy, he trained at the renowned Juilliard School in New York. Fresh from this competitive forcing house, he went to London and was amazed when he played with musicians there. In rehearsals he found that his fellow players would suggest changes by saying not "I think ..." or "Let's ..." but "I would have thought ..."

This gently probing language, Sennett saw, had a magical effect. It opened up "an indeterminate mutual space, the space in which strangers dwell with one another." This space was a lifesaver, he came to feel, in a world that throws strangers together in vast cities, or hidden behind avatars online, and asks them to be civil to each other. In these communities of token commitment, where the social contract amounts to letting others exist, we must forge a basic commonality. We do not need to like each other, but we had best keep our less convivial impulses to ourselves. "The social engine is oiled," Sennett concluded, "when people do not behave too emphatically."

Along with tenses and aspects, verbs have moods. These

make known the necessity, likelihood or reality of an event. The indicative mood, the standard way of saying that something has happened, is clear and the style guides prefer it. But used too much, as Sennett suggests, it makes a fetish of the real, the things that have actually happened or definitely will. Its blunt imparting of facts can feel unsociable—as if what you are saying goes without saying and the reader had better take it or leave it.

Today, in our feverish public sphere, the indicative reigns. There is little need for modal verbs in the strident op-ed piece written as clickbait, or the pointless, self-consuming anger of its below-the-line comments. Ours is an era of *truthiness*. The American comedian Stephen Colbert coined this word to mean the truth that is known intuitively, regardless of the evidence. It often comes with an appeal to *the real world*, within which the person who denies the truthiness is supposedly refusing to live. That person is urged to come out of their airy, privileged bubble and face facts—facts that, denuded of nuance, speak for themselves, except that no one can agree on them.

We are going to need more precise language than this to get our heads round ever more untidy and bewildering reality. "How to explain," as Maggie Nelson writes in *The Argonauts*, "in a culture frantic for resolution, that sometimes the shit stays messy?" We don't just live in the indicative anymore, if we ever did. If our world of data overload and infinite choice should teach us anything, it is that billions of lives, billions of different and valid realities, are being lived all at once. There is only one "real world" and we all have to live in it.

As soon as class is over, before they have even left their seats, my students reach for their phones to see what has been happening in these billions of other lives. As they walk the corridors, the wireless routers in the dropped ceilings send pinging alerts to their devices. They dwell in this touchless non-space, the workings of which are a mystery to them, but which still eats up their lives and regurgitates them as a waking dream, or makes them feel that better lives are being lived somewhere just out of reach. It all brings to mind the title of a Milan Kundera novel: *Life is Elsewhere*.

They need, it seems to me, verb forms that can be honest about their perplexity. These verb forms would make them see that they have choices, that life is not elsewhere but is theirs now to live, and that the future may be hard and confusing but is theirs to make. Instead of imposing a false clarity on uncertainty—with truthiness, or factoids available at the click of a mouse—these verb forms would help them to convey uncertainty as cleanly as they can. For without that uncertainty there is no freedom and no possibility—only depressive fatalism, a stunned surrendering to circumstance.

Help is at hand. To convey uncertainty cleanly, without over-depending on cumbersome modals, another mood is available. The subjunctive is sometimes thought old-fashioned. We rarely use it in speech, so when we write *if it be true* or *if she were right* it looks interestingly "wrong"—or, at least, unmistakably like writing. In the subjunctive we use odd-looking verb endings like *It is vital that he avoid swearing on air.* Or we seem to shift tenses (but don't). *When divvying up the restaurant bill, he demanded that the dessert-eaters pay more.*

But the subjunctive also lets us say sparingly whether something that hasn't happened is possible, desirable, necessary or real. Modal verbs do this as well, but the subjunctive calls up this alternative reality with elegant brevity, without always needing an auxiliary verb or a relative clause. The word *lest* is sometimes thought fussy, but *lest he get upset* is less fussy than *so that he doesn't get upset*. The subjunctive adds a layer of conjecture to a sentence without weighing it down. It makes the possible seem plausible. Too many modal *coulds* and *mights* leave writing sounding fuzzy. The subjunctive sounds clear and sure. It lets you smoothly sidestep linear time, and the obstinacies of the real, and enter a second life of the might-be or might-have-been. The unlived life is also life.

•

In his novel *Mason & Dixon*, Thomas Pynchon tells the story of Charles Mason and Jeremiah Dixon's surveying expeditions in America just before the Revolutionary War. To resolve America's disputed borders, they draw their famous Mason–Dixon Line. It aims to disenchant the land, to impose a straight line where none exists in nature, to tame what Pynchon calls "the realm of the Subjunctive." The Native Americans of the Ohio River valley live in this realm, divided by an invisible membrane from "our number'd and dreamless Indicative." For Pynchon the subjunctive means living with possibility. It stands for the untamed reality that surveyors destroy by drawing lines. America should never forget that it is a "Rubbish-Tip for subjunctive hopes." These hopes are all that save us from "the bare mortal World that is our home, and our Despair."

We need the subjunctive lest we shoehorn life's intricacies into a shoe that is too neat, small and painful. Using it well lets us inhabit different ways of looking at the world. And here lies the power not just of the subjunctive but of verbs in all their forms and moods. Verbs are for painting life both as we are forced to live it and as it might be lived. Nouns find words for things in the world; verbs weave their own worlds out of words.

We need verbs not just to say what has happened but to pass through different levels of reality. Verbs relate events but also rumors, surmises, dreams and desires. A friend once told me, when declaring that she had altered her view on something, that "changing your mind is an occupational hazard of thought." True enough, and this irreversible side effect of thinking is what verbs are for. Verbs map the mutability not only of the world but also of our minds.

A sentence brings together a noun, which names a thing, with a verb, which says something about that thing. That is all a sentence needs: everything else is optional. If you put the right nouns and verbs in the right slots, the other words fall into place around them. By varying the types of noun and verb, you give your sentences a grain and texture that begins to approximate life. The task is to layer reality without extracting too much verbal heat—to be intricate but not convoluted, and just as simple as is needed, but no more.

•

Nouns and verbs are the two poles of the sentence. Nouns keep it still; verbs make it move. But nouns and verbs also live on a continuum. At one end, the nouniest nouns are the nominalizations, the names for abstract, inert things. At the other end, the verbiest verbs are finite and transitive, showing animated subjects acting on the world. In the middle, the nouny verbs mix with the verby nouns. *To be* is nouny because it says that something is equal to or has the quality of something else. *To have* is almost as nouny—its literal meaning, "to hold," having long been submerged by its abstract meanings, such as "to relate to" or "to own as a trait." Linking verbs are nouny when they form phrases ending in nouns, like *remain a mystery* or *make a decision*. Gerunds are nouny—actual nouns, in fact, albeit ones with verbs buried inside them.

Participles are verby because beneath the adjective burns the verbal heat of an action. Infinitives are nouny when they form the subject: *To cry* is to know that you are alive. But they are verby when they form the predicate: I started *to cry*. The bare infinitive (without the *to*) adds a one-word boost of verbiness, often at the sentence's end. You did nothing but *cry*. You'd better *leave*. I will *return*. You needn't *bother*.

Every sentence has to mix the right blend of nouns and verbs. The precise mix depends on what you want to say and how. A year into the Second World War, Virginia Woolf wrote this defiant sentence in her journal: "Thinking is my fighting." Even though that doesn't have what style guides tend to like—a concrete subject and strong verbs—it has a low rumble of energy running through it. Why? Because, apart from its possessive pronoun, it consists wholly of verbs or verbals. Verbs bring a sentence to life whatever form they take. Weighing down your sentence with nouns is always bad. But verbs, behind which you can never hide because they make you say what the subjects of your sentences are doing, are always good.

4.

Nothing Like a Windowpane

Or how to say wondrous things with plain words

In September 1939 a ten-year-old boy was evacuated from London's East End to the English countryside. At the village school he was told to write an essay on "a bird and a beast." "The bird that I am going to write about is the owl," began this exiled urbanite. "I do not know much about the owl, so I will go on to the beast which I am going to choose. It is the cow. The cow is a mammal. It has six sides—right, left, an upper and below. At the back it has a tail on which hangs a brush. With this it sends the flies away so that they do not fall into the milk. The head is for the purpose of growing horns and so that the mouth can be somewhere. The horns are to butt with, and the mouth is to moo with ... When it is hungry it moos, and when it says nothing it is because its inside is all full up with grass."

The following month this essay was read out on the BBC's nine o'clock news, in an item about evacuees. Listening in was a senior civil servant, Ernest Gowers. Gowers felt that, despite the young writer's considerable non-expertise in owls and cows, he knew what he wanted to say and had not littered his prose with the befogging abstractions of officialese. Whether a cow has six sides is moot. But its mouth does have to be somewhere, and it does use it to moo with. These were facts, plainly put.

In 1948 Gowers published a book, *Plain Words*. Conceived as a writing guide for civil servants, it taught them to avoid using lots of *heretos* and *herewiths*, and to eschew finger-wagging fussiness like *Receipt of your letter is acknowledged* or *You may consider the matter closed*. But it also found a general readership, becoming the fastest-selling book ever issued by His Majesty's Stationery Office. It told these readers how to write in a way that was clear, simple and sincere. Included, as an exemplar, was the schoolboy's essay.

"Writing is an instrument for conveying ideas from one mind to another," Gowers wrote. Sound advice if you are a civil servant writing to confused citizens about their entitlements and obligations. Less so, perhaps, if you want to write in a way that is melodic, memorable and life-enhancing. That ten-year-old's essay was clear enough, but its leaden literalism would soon begin to grate.

For behind the ideal of "plain English" lies a mistrust of writing that goes back to Plato. Writing should be unseen, it declares, a transparent vessel empty of all but the author's thoughts, which can then be poured lightly into the reader's lap. One should notice the words no more than someone looking through glass notices the glass. George Orwell, in his essay "Why I Write," gave this idea its epigram: "Good prose is like a windowpane."

•

Except that you do notice glass. Picture an English window in 1946, when Orwell wrote that sentence. It would be smeared with grime from smoke and coal dust and, since houses were damp and windows single-glazed, wont to mist and ice over. The glass might still be cracked from air-raid gunfire or bombings, or covered with strips of paper and shatterproof coating to protect people from flying shards. An odd metaphor to use, perhaps, for clear writing.

Behind the windowpane theory of prose lies a trace of puritan pride, a sense that the reader will be purified by a clean, sinewy style as by an early morning run and a cold shower. "The great enemy of clear language is insincerity," Orwell wrote. For him plain writing went with plain speaking, and insincere writing spat out tired idioms "like a cuttlefish spurting out ink." Bad ideas are the bedfellows of bad prose. Fake thoughts mean fake words.

Some of this is true but none of it is a good way of learning how to write a sentence. More ethical demand than helpful advice, it forces you back on to your own reserves of wisdom and authenticity. It assumes you always know what you mean and what you want to say. It blames bad writing on laziness and dishonesty, when a likelier culprit is lack of skill. If you ordered me to make a blancmange, all I could come up with would be a gloopy, inedible mess—not because I am lazy or dishonest, but because, although I have some vague idea that it needs sugar, cornflour and boiled milk, I don't know how to make a blancmange.

And should you always be clear about what you are going to say before you say it? More useful might be the way of classical rhetoric: learn how a good sentence sounds and mimic it. Instead of draining some finite pool of sense, write in a way that engenders sense out of nothing. That is how Shakespeare learned to write at grammar school—rote learning the art of verbal ornament, getting to know words as sounds and shapes before they calcified into meaning. The rhetorician sees meaning as something reached by tasting and relishing the words, not by trying to make the writing invisible. She seeks sincerity, but comes at it from an angle, and aims at the truth, but with glancing blows. She wants to forge reality through words, not just gaze at it blankly through a window.

Orwell, it turns out, is an outlier. Few skilled writers subscribe to his windowpane theory. They think of all writing, however firmly factual, as creative writing. They are happy to let the word order press meanings on them, to find out what they want to say by saying it. Like the psychoanalyst Adam Phillips, declaring his distaste for hard Freudian theory and his preference for using words themselves as the laboratory for thought, they are "more interested in sentences than ideas." And they know that verbal economy is just as affected as the purplest prose. To write in the plain style, you must learn its tricks. The plain style is just that—a style.

•

In his book *Barbarian Days*, on his life as a surfer, William Finnegan writes that the aesthetics of surfing are about how nonchalantly you solve the problem each wave presents. The surfer styles it out by making it all look natural, when every branch of physics is screaming at him to fall over. He must stay elegantly upright while climbing the wall of a wave and dancing along it and then, before it breaks, he must handle the pullout as if it were a perfectly placed full stop. "Casual power, the proverbial grace under pressure, these were our beau ideals," Finnegan writes. "Pull into a heaving barrel, come out cleanly. Act like you've been there before."

Finnegan calls this surfer aesthetic, in a description that many writers would happily apply to their own lonely obsession with the perfect form of words, a "special brand of monomania." The surfer's search for the perfect response to a wave needs to be a self-rewarding pursuit, because surfing is not a spectator sport. Surfers are too far out, where the big waves are, to be seen properly from the shore, and other surfers are too busy with their own boards to be closely watching others.

Writing is more of a spectator sport than surfing. But still there is a sense, especially among plain stylists, that its effortfulness, and the writer's psychic need for that effort to be noted and rewarded, must be hidden. A sentence in the plain style feels undersold, rather like the surfer's studiedly casual riding of a wave. Much work goes into making it seem as if the writer, like the surfer, has been here before. But the plain stylist still knows, just as the surfer does, that style is everything.

•

The plain stylist thinks it better to be bold and almost right than timid and never wrong. So here is a bold claim. The first master of the English plain style was William Tyndale, translator of the Bible. All a modern reader need do is straighten out his spelling and she will feel quite at home in his prose—more so than in the King James Bible, with its orotund *thees* and *verilys*. Much of the King James was taken straight from Tyndale anyway. If you want to write a short, simple, sweet-sounding sentence, Tyndale will show you how.

Now and then I slip off to Liverpool's Metropolitan Cathedral, just across the road from where I work, and sit at the back while a service is on. My Catholicism is long-lapsed but I like the way the Dean's soft Scouse resounds in the circular nave, bringing out Tyndale's rhythms beautifully. Meanwhile, in the city center, there is a man who stands at a busking pitch, reading from the New Testament with a radio mic wrapped round his head. His voice is a nasal drone and passersby shout the odd disobliging thing and throw him off his stride. But the biblical cadences survive even this sterile setting. Sometimes I linger by a shop window just to listen to him.

I used to wonder who this man reminded me of, and then it came to me. He was the grown-up version of the little boy playing Linus van Pelt, reading from St. Luke in *A Charlie Brown Christmas*. Chris Shea, that lispy seven-year-old child actor, had no great ear for the words either. But the scene in which Linus walks to the center of the school stage, asks for the lights to be dimmed and declaims the Nativity story is renowned for making viewers weep.

And there were in the same region shepherds abiding in the field, and watching their flock by night. What is it about Tyndale's words, read aloud, that can ease breaking hearts, fill in for wordless grief and reduce even unbelievers like me to tears? His sentences are strong yet pliant, syntactically clean yet emotionally rich. They mix vigor and (oddly, even in the fire-and-brimstone bits) gentleness. With these words Tyndale risked his life and then lost it. In 1537, a year after he was burned at the stake, a complete English Bible, two thirds of it his, appeared at the King's behest. Those deathless sentences, which once had to be smuggled into the country in single sheets hidden in cargoes of woad or sacks of flour, refused to die.

•

Tyndale's writing works like heightened and amplified speech. His native Gloucestershire was known for its traveling preachers and its proverbs, religious and otherwise. He has the same ear for vivid sayings, pitched just above normal talk, such as *the salt of the earth* or *the powers that be* or *in the twinkling of an eye.* Just as a proverb does, he takes the spoken word and moves it up a notch, while keeping the pulse and beat of speech.

Tyndale's Bible was meant to be read aloud. Not only does it sound as good as it reads, it also sounds in the head *as* you read. No one knows how far into the history of reading people started doing it silently. In his *Confessions*, St. Augustine is astonished to see Ambrose, Bishop of Milan, read without moving his lips. Plutarch said the same about Julius Caesar and Alexander the Great, and characters in Greek tragedies read letters silently. But Augustine was still right to be astonished—as we should be, still.

One of the many forgotten miracles of silent reading is that it preserves the traces of reading aloud. Silent readers minutely move the nerves, and sometimes the muscles, in their throats, as if they were about to speak. However fast they read, they subvocalize, hearing the words in their heads as the brain sends signals to the vocal cords. Like a musician who scans a score and hears the notes, they read with their ears and mouths as well as their eyes. Nouny writing is hard to read because it cannot be heard. It just welds together boilerplate phrases with none of the natural verbal vigor of speech. A sentence is meant to give off sound.

I like my sentences to look the same as they speak. I steer clear of contractions, like *No.* or *Ltd*, and spell out numbers up to a hundred, because otherwise the reader has to think for a micro-moment about how to turn that symbol into sound. I avoid the en dash if it requires the reader to silently say the word *to*, as in *the 1939–1945 war*. I shun that forward-slanting line, the solidus, because it means the reader has to say *slash* in her head when it is not on the page. Eccentricities of mine, perhaps. But if the reader can't hear the words, how can she pace out the beat of a sentence?

Many accidental sound jangles are solved by reading your sentences aloud. Today I saw a line in a newspaper about a man who came "from the glitzy Riviera area on the southern coastline." If the writer had read that aloud, he would have learned that you cannot actually *say* "Riviera area." Nor do you need to, because the Riviera is already an area (and it means "coastline," so he didn't need that word either). Reading the words aloud obliges you to renotice what you have said. Having to share those words, even if you are alone and it is just with the surrounding air, makes you more fastidious about owning and standing by them.

But this is no solve-all. When you speak your own words you already know what you meant, and you augment that meaning by accenting and stressing, speaking faster or slower, higher or lower—all potent slayers of opacity and ambiguity. Better, if you can bear it, to get someone to read out your sentences for you. If they stumble over a word, revisit it. Your sentence has been found out.

Sentences should be as much like speech as you can make them—so long as you remember that they are nothing like speech. Writing needs to retain the loose shapes of talk, its rhythmic curves and breathing pauses, but overlay them with the tighter shapes of writing. Tyndale's sentences feel like that. They land in this sweet spot, this fertile ground between writing and talk. They have godly grandeur but vernacular ease, the stateliness of liturgy but the artlessness of speech. A sentence should ring in the head but be wrought like writing.

•

Tyndale has a trick to make his prose more speech-like: he uses short words. The ancient Hebrew and Greek of the Bible have few long words, nor does the language Tyndale relies on: Old English. (In fact, words in Old English were not always short, because its inflections added syllables. But words that derive from Old English, shorn of these endings as they were by Tyndale's time, are.) Old English words like *ooze* and *spit* retain an onomatopoeia that perhaps all words once had. Old English *shut* and *shun* sound out their meanings; Middle English *close* and *avoid* do not. Old English verbs, like *flee*, *beckon*, *bless*, *chide* and *chew*, are full of, to use an Old English noun, *pith*.

Old English words also feel close to speech. Normally each letter relates to a single sound, with few of the silent letters and phonetic oddities of newer words. Longer words like *friendship* and *elsewhere* seem composed of monosyllables, so they fold out into parts in your head. Words like *bookhoard* and *starcraft* have a blunt lyricism not shared by their modern equivalents (*library* and *astronomy*). Old English kennings, the compound nouns used as poetic synonyms—*whale road* for sea, *bone house* for body, *battle light* for sword—are plain-spoken poetry.

In the centuries after the Norman Conquest, tens of thousands of words came into English from French, Latin, Greek and other languages. These words tend to be longer than Old English ones and more genteel. *Conclusion*, not *end*; *assist*, not *help*; *perspire*, not *sweat*; *deceased*, not *dead*. But they also add economical exactitude to the language, because words like *orthodox* or *imperceptible* say with one word what once needed several.

Old English words are still used far more than these Romance words, even though there are far more of the latter. Since Old English accounts for the basic mortar of a sentence like pronouns, articles and prepositions, you cannot write English without Old English words. And you can have a good stab at writing English using them alone. Old English is the tongue of a preliterate people, whose lives turn around family, tribe and the elemental world that we know as children—of *night* and *day*, *cold* and *dark*, *breath* and *life*, *meat* and *bread*, *hunger* and *thirst*.

Tyndale prefers Old English solidity to Latinate remoteness. *Freedom*, not *liberty*; *brotherly*, not *fraternal*; *folk*, not *people*; *foe*, not *enemy*. But not always. Sometimes he renders the same Hebrew word in both Old and Latinate English. *Kindred* and *relation*, *house* and *habitation*, *greeting* and *salutation*. And he puts long words at the start and end of sentences, for weight. His first translation of Matthew invited us to *Behold the lilies of the field*. Then he changed it to the inexplicably better *Consider the lilies of the field*. Where John Wycliffe's earlier Bible has *Blessed be peaceable men*, Tyndale's has *Blessed are the peacemakers*, which opens out like a fan. One long word in a sentence of short ones draws just the right amount of attention to itself.

•

Using mostly short words in a sentence has a happy side effect: a richer pattern of sounds. Speech is a bodily thing. We feel the words in our mouths as we shape our jaws, teeth and lips around them. These chunks of sonic air are made by the same body parts with which we breathe, taste and kiss. By shutting our lips and humming, or closing the throat, or using our tongues, we make the semi-blocked sounds called consonants. By opening our mouths, we make the unblocked sounds called vowels.

The vowel sound of a syllable is the basic unit of speech. A consonant cannot be fully voiced without it. Every voice is an exhaled breath; every unconstricted sound that the breath makes is a vowel sound. So vowels have more vocal heft than consonants. Professional singers, rehearsing a song, will often just sing the vowel sounds, because they know that is where the emotional power resides. In operatic arias the singer lingers on the vowels, floating the tune on her outward breath.

Poets love these strong and varied vowel sounds. Don Paterson says that poetry differs from ordinary language in the prominence it gives to the vowel. Poems get their music from the vowelly chewiness of single words, and from the dancing cadences of the words joined together. We notice the obvious magic of cadence, but not always the subtler magic of vowels. Poems are felt and we feel them most in our mouths, where the vowel sounds meet. Words are only flat on the page. In the mouth and in the head, where silent reading sounds, they are solid and alive.

The vowel sounds carry the weight of rises and falls in pitch and changes in stress, and so carry the mood. The monophthongs of *but, come* or *lip* feel abrupt. The longer vowel sounds and diphthongs of *need* or *ground* feel slower and more settled. Vowel sounds vary from the wide-open *ah* (heard in baby words like *mama* and *dada)* to *ee* (near the front of the mouth), *I* (the top) and *oo* (the back). Sentences that make lots of different vowel sounds are nicely mouth-stretching. *Those yellow-tinted shades are so cool.*

Varied vowel sounds are not just useful for poets; they bring all writing to life. Lots of short words in a sentence fattens the vowel sounds and cuts down on schwa. Schwa is that little, indistinct *uh* sound in unstressed syllables—such as the *a* in *above*, or *sofa*. Schwa is the most common sound in English, although you barely hear it, because it doesn't shape the mouth. It lurks in long words like *monopolization*, bridging the consonants and making the vowel sound all but vanish. When you remove almost all a vowel's energy, schwa is what is left. The monosyllabic phrases uttered by Tyndale's Jesus—*Let this cup pass from me; Not as I will, but as thou wilt; Take up thy bed and walk*—are free of schwa. Slightly chewier to say than normal speech, they shape the lips and jaw until they become a bit of a mouthful but never too much of one.

Short words have something else going for them. A sentence has more sonic force if there are more stressed than unstressed syllables. When we speak, we stress one syllable of each word. Even polysyllabic words stress only one key syllable, so the more long words there are in a sentence, the fewer stresses it has. Hence poetic lines composed of short words are "long," because with all the stresses, and the mouth-stretching vowels, they take longer to say. Not many writers bother to count the number of stressed syllables or even strive to vary the vowel sounds in their sentences. But there is an easy way to get a higher count of both: use short words.

When the vowel sounds vary and there are lots of stressed syllables, each word seems distinct from its neighbors. Every word counts. Most competent writers know how to make every word count in a basic way, by not lazily repeating words—the most common symptom of absentminded writing. But fewer writers notice a bigger problem: repeated sounds. The careful ones notice not just words but word kernels, the sounds that live inside words. Unintended echoes of prefixes and suffixes like *con-*, *-ess* or *-ation* make for schwa-sodden prose. Academic writing's clankiest sounds come from its *-tate* verbs, like *necessitate* and *facilitate*, and its *-shun* nouns, like *evaluation* and *function*. The critic Richard Lanham calls such writing "mumblespeak" because the sounds are insufficiently distinct and you hear them as muffled noise-making. You can do a global search for *-tate* and *-shun* endings in your writing and cull them. But the quickest cure for mumblespeak is shorter words.

Cut syllables where you can. *Blindfolded*: *blindfold*. *Unnecessary*: *needless*. *Begin*: *start*. *Eyesight*: *sight*. *Previously*: *hitherto*. Genteel words suffer from syllable flab. *Individual*: *person*. *Sufficient*: *enough*. *Ascertain*: *learn*. *Shape* is better than *structure* because it has one less syllable (and no schwa), and feels more solid than *structure*. *Let* is better than *allow*, because it is one less syllable and does not need to be paired with *to*. And it is sometimes worth reviving now uncommon words like *frit*, *atop* and *writ* (as a past participle) because they save syllables and cut schwa.

Modern Bible versions are often more literal translations of the Hebrew and Greek than Tyndale. But they have forgotten the power of sentences as vowelly mouthfuls with lots of stresses. Tyndale's *I pray thee have me excused* becomes *Please accept my apologies*. *Let not your hearts be troubled* becomes *Do not be worried or upset*. *Neither cast ye your pearls before swine* becomes *Do not throw your pearls to the pigs*. The words have lost the tune that made them stay in the head: the chewy vowel music.

•

In Tyndale's sentences, every word earns its keep like a stake beaten hard into the ground. And yet the words also feel warmly linked, woven into lovely, bright little phrases such as *In him we live, move and have our being*. His sentences read so well because the words each have their own separate lives but still relate to each other as kith and kin. The words are all discretely meaningful but they come together as more than the sum of their parts.

Poets know how to make words distinct from each other, by varying the vowel sounds. But they also know how to bring words together, by using assonance, alliteration and rhyme. Prose can use these acoustic patterns to marry words as well, albeit more subliminally. But mostly it links words by repetition—of both words and syntactical forms. Syntactical repetition, which puts similar ideas into similar shapes, is called parallelism. Parts of speech, for instance, tend to pair off with their own kind: adverb with adverb, adjective with adjective, preposition with preposition, article with article, noun with noun. Sand grains on a beach are *infinitesimally small in the singular* yet *immeasurably vast in the plural*.

Tyndale's parallel patterns feel just the right mix of artful and natural. *Ask, and ye shall obtain; seek, and ye shall find; knock, and the door will be opened to you*. These patterns make more than just pleasing shapes; they throw the sentence forward in rhythmic pulses and illuminate its meaning. The ancient art of rhetoric was all about fashioning these light-shedding patterns with words. Tyndale is fond of a trick the Greeks called *polyptoton*, repeating a word but in a different form or part of speech. I have been a *stranger* in a *strange* land. Give us this *day* our *daily* bread. *Judge* not, that ye be not *judged*. Accidental repetition sounds clunky and careless; intentional repetition sounds musical and meant.

The writer and musician David Teems points out that Tyndale grew up right on the Welsh border and may have gotten some of the Welsh language into his bones. In Welsh, as in all Celtic languages, words have a warm affiliation, "a peace one word makes with its fellow." If the end of one word causes sonic friction with the start of the next, Welsh has the built-in remedy of soft mutations. It slurs its sounds for music's sake, smoothing a *t* into a *d*, or a *c* into a *g* (hence "Welcome to Wales" road signs say *Croeso i Gymru* not *Croeso i Cymru*). As the poet Gwyneth Lewis says, Welsh has "a softness going around the corners," so when words touch each other they "rub some of the molecules off." The speaker cares how the words fall on the ears. Welsh is a consensual language, a necessity in small valley villages where people cannot just speak their mind and then burn their boats.

Used to seeing them written down, we think of words as autonomous entities, divided from other words by equidistant white space. But in speech, words are sound shapes running pell-mell into each other. In 1929 an American missionary, Frank Laubach, arrived at Lake Lanao on the island of Mindanao in the Philippines to start work among the Moro people. He wanted to devise a written form of their language, Maranaw, so he could teach them to read and write. But none of the Moros could tell him where one word began and ended. They did not know the word for "go," only that *Where are you going?* was *Andakasoong?* Laubach had to work out for himself, by trial and error, that *anda* was "where," *ka* was "you," and *soong* was "go."

Speech is not made of words separated by silence, but of sound streams separated by breathing pauses. We hear, first of all, the kernels of words—vowel-consonant bits of acoustic energy. Then we hear not the words but the fluid phrases into which they form. Speech comes in spurts of sound, about two seconds long, called intonation units, which stress one key word and then end with a tiny pause before moving on to the next two-second spurt. Speech has to divide up into these little bundles to be understood.

In writing, intonation units are not so crucial, because a reader has more time than a listener to untangle the words. But a written sentence still reads easier and better if it divides into these little phrases, sayable in a single breath. Writing like this gives off some of the spontaneous musical rightness of speech—even if those intonation units are then linked up, as they should be, with more crafted, artful writing. A sentence split into two-second phrases gives off sound, the sound of someone speaking.

•

Tyndale links up his intonation units with parataxis (Greek for "arrangement alongside"). This means joining clauses simply by juxtaposing them—with a plain *and*, *but*, *then* or *so*, or with mere punctuation. Its opposite is hypotaxis ("arrangement under"), which joins relative and subordinate clauses to a main clause.

Parataxis is plain, additive, egalitarian. Each clause has equal billing and makes sense if detached from the rest of the sentence. Hypotaxis is nuanced, layered, hierarchical. The subordinate clauses are servants to the main clause, and the sentence makes sense only when you have untied it all. Latin prefers hypotaxis. Ancient Hebrew and Greek, and Old English, prefer parataxis. In Tyndale's Bible this means lots of gently undulating *ands. For this thy brother was dead, and is alive again; and was lost, and is found.*

Hypotaxis links its clauses subtly, carefully leading the reader through a sentence's graduated parts. It sounds judicious, thought through, unruffled. It would never be caught out saying anything naive or off-guard or unfiltered by its author's cool intelligence. As a young scholar I lived off hypotaxis as I lived off caffeine and crisps. Look at me, calmly putting my clauses in rank order and holding them in balance!

Subtle writing needs hypotaxis—only the most inept writers give equal weight to every idea—and subtle writers can subordinate clauses in barely noticeable ways. *The more I saw my life as a stranger might see it, the glummer I got.* Often they subordinate invisibly by leaving out the relative pronouns. *I changed the dress [that] I was wearing so it did not clash with my shoes.*

But hypotaxis can be overdone. A long chain of hypotactic sentences feels leached of life, its motion halted by hierarchy. If the subordinate clauses extend into ten words or more, and become longer than the main clauses, reading them is a grind. A sentence stuffed with subordination is trying to spell out all the links but is just giving the reader more to do. She has to think ahead and back to unpick all the *whiches, whens, ifs* and *thats*.

This kind of writing wants to be read as carefully as it has been written. Do you know your reader well enough to ask that of her? If not, then parataxis throws a stranger a rope. Sometimes this can be as simple as not starting so many sentences with *although* or *since*. Start instead with the main clause, followed by *but* or *so*, and the reader will see the key point before its qualification and be grateful.

Parataxis feels simpler and less studied, closer to the slowly snowballing rhythms of speech. Most speakers, and their listeners, cannot hold subordinations in their heads. So they leave the qualification until the next sentence, which is why so many spoken sentences begin with *but*. The easy transitions of parataxis suit closing sections of writing, as they hasten the reader to the end once the subtler points are done.

Parataxis is not just easier to read. It actually strengthens the links between clauses. The critic Erich Auerbach, in his book *Mimesis*, pointed out that "he opened his eyes and was struck" has more force than "when he opened his eyes, he was struck" or "upon opening his eyes, he was struck ..." Just setting clauses alongside each other means the reader makes the link for herself. Parataxis is simple: child writers, before they learn other ways of joining up words, link them with *and*. But it also treats your reader like a grown-up by leaving him with more to do. Correlation may not be causation, but sometimes putting two and two together is enough. *I ate that chicken madras and I felt ill.*

Hypotaxis, with its finely sieved distinctions, keeps clauses apart. Parataxis, with its warm communities of words, brings them together. The *and* of ancient Hebrew that appears so often in Tyndale's Bible was not even a discrete word but a sound, *waw*, stuck on to the first word of the clause. *Waw* means "hook" and its early Semitic pictograph was a Y-shape, meant to resemble a tent peg. Parataxis was not just a way of linking words; it was a way of thinking about everything in the world as snugly linked, tent-pegged tight together.

•

Parataxis is both a style and a state of mind. In the Bible, as in epics like the *Iliad* and the *Odyssey*, the style is paratactic because everything in the world is seen as organically or magically connected, with all its mortals watched over by God, or by the gods. We no longer live in this simple, joined-up world. But it may be worth reinhabiting it, and that paratactic state of mind, for the reader's sake, it being quite hard to overuse that generous, openhanded little word, *and*.

The plain style uses parataxis because its author is willing to sound slightly less clever than she is. She has agreed not to cloud her prose with a nit-picking nuance that is really a tacit avowal of her own cleverness. You and I know, the plain stylist says to the reader, that the world is not quite this straightforward. But let us pretend that it is for the duration of these words, so we can hack out a clearing amid the undergrowth of reality and, together, look around.

When you have the confidence just to notice the world and assemble what you have seen into paratactic shapes, the worst awkwardnesses of writing disappear. So much uncongenial writing comes from the fear of boring others with the obvious. Scared of sounding banal, we muddy our prose and it ends up sounding muddy *and* banal. The best way to unkink a twisted train of thought or to massage a misshapen piece of logic is simply to say what you have seen and let the reader join the dots.

Adam Gopnik says that he made a breakthrough as a young writer when he saw how far he could get just by setting down faux-naif declaratives and seeing where they took him, since "wherever you were going, the power of sentences lay in their simple additive observations." He wrote this opening: "I am a student at the Institute of Fine Arts, and I work part time at the Frick Art Reference Library." After that easy bit of parataxis he just carried on from there. This faux-naif voice he called "a well-wishingness, a willingness to be wide-eyed in the face of new material even at the risk of seeming a little silly or insufficiently self-protective and knowing." Good writing is done with a cold eye but an open heart.

•

The plain style is paratactic because parataxis uses fewer words, and the plain style pares down wherever it can. "If it is possible to cut a word out, always cut it out," Orwell advised. Or: *If you can cut a word, do.* English offers limitless options for pruning phrases and chopping words. *Close to: near. Have to: must. The ways in which: how. More difficult: harder. If she had: had she. Whether or not: whether.* Save words by avoiding polite evasions. *Has a life-limiting illness: is dying. Passed away: died. Loss of life: death.*

Adverbs and prepositions can be cut from verbal phrases with no loss of meaning, such as *up* (*fold up, warm up*), *back* (*cut back, revert back*), *out* (*miss out, try out*), *down* (*cut down, sit down*) and *ever* (*rarely ever, seldom ever*). Some words just grow pointlessly into phrases, like *book in advance (book), from noon onwards (from noon)* or *forty years old (forty)*. Stating negatives more affirmatively cuts words and syllables. *Cannot do anything: can do nothing. Does not need: needs no. Not successful: failed.* Taking up too much of your reader's life, by having him read sentences barnacled with needless words, is an ungenerous act. Cutting words is a silent, invisible gift to that reader—and a thankless task, inevitably, since no one but you knows you have done it.

More than that, though: cutting words is also writing. We make meaning not just by adding words but by taking them away. The computer key we know best of all, the backspace, is our friend disguised as our enemy. Michelangelo said that David was hidden in that rough block of marble all along. The art of it was freeing the body from within by removing the superfluous stone. All that sculpture's flawless detail—the tensed neck, the bulging veins on the hands, the twist of the torso and the curve of the hips so frugally conveying that a moment of repose is about to turn into action—was made only by gouging out, flaking off and chipping away. Cutting words has this same creative quality. It seems to liberate a meaning that the writer was not aware of but that was waiting there to be found. Distilling prose, like boiling down a sauce, releases its real flavor and its true essence.

The architect Mies van der Rohe put this truth in its simplest and thus aptest form: "Less is more." "Elegance is refusal," said Coco Chanel, just a little less succinctly. "Only the superfluous is sordid," wrote Boris Pasternak in *Doctor Zhivago*. The old are often caricatured as rambling and verbose, but this is certainly not true of writers, who tend to pare down their prose as they mature. At the age of seventy, Stephen Sondheim said: "'Less is more' is a lesson learned with difficulty. As you get older, you pay more attention to it—that's why composers end up writing string quartets."

•

The plain stylist singles out two word types as especially ripe for cutting: adverbs and adjectives. These parts of speech often betray a nerviness that the point has not been made. Or they are trying to prop up a verb or noun too weak to stand up for itself, or muscle in when the verb or noun is strong enough on its own. In the parallel reality of amateur fiction, radios blare *loudly*, hands caress *gently* and characters saunter *nonchalantly*. Surprises, meanwhile, are *unexpected*, flames are *burning* and fists are *closed*. (A fist that isn't closed is just a hand.)

The worst offenders are degree adverbs, which specify to what extent a verb applies. The worst of these are mere intensifiers, like *immensely* or *extremely*. Intensifiers have been declining in use for hundreds of years. The number of *very*s in Jane Austen's novels sounds absurd to modern ears until we learn to tune them out, as her contemporaries presumably did. Double-adverb phrases like *terribly quickly* or *really messily* are *nearly always* superfluous.

Writers unconvinced of their own arguments betray this with hedging adverbs (*arguably, generally*) or blustering ones (*surely, certainly*) or both. Adverbs that signal continuity or frequency— *usually, still, ever*—can be cut if the verb alone suggests, as it often does, its own sense of continuity or frequency. *Currently* can be cut if you are writing in the present tense, which conveys currency perfectly well. The adverb *so* can also often be cut, as indeed can *also* and *often*—and, indeed, *indeed*.

Words are our first and fiercest addiction. They spew out of us so freely that habit takes over. The same crutch words and verbal offcuts help us to rustle up a sentence easily. Adverbs and adjectives come together in the trite pairings known as collocations: *scantily clad, finely balanced, thinly veiled, eagerly anticipated*. Adjectives and nouns form the same tired couplings: *rich tapestry, daunting prospect, chilling foretaste, veritable cornucopia*. Why are these collocations so hard to kill off? Because, in the pressed and weary writer's head, the two words turned into one word, and that single word nestled down inside the sentence until it was invisible.

•

The French theorist Roland Barthes hated adjectives. The hatred was personal. In 1968 he was teaching at the École Pratique des Hautes Études in Paris, and the student unrest of the May *événements* made him uneasy. He preferred the studied precision of writing to the sloganeering speeches of the Sorbonne. He began spending long periods away from Paris, teaching in Morocco. As an undeclared gay man he also found the bars and saunas of Tangier and Marrakesh a liberation. He felt free there, where "neither *this* nor *that* was returned in the form of a fine adjective: it never occurred to them to *gloss* me."

In his anti-memoir, *Roland Barthes* by Roland Barthes, he writes of his desire "to abolish—in oneself, between oneself and others— *adjectives*: a relationship which adjectivizes is on the side of the image, on the side of domination, of death." Loving someone deeply, Barthes felt, meant not trying to decipher or possess them with description. An adjective applied to someone else, whether it aimed to flatter or wound, was about asserting control, pinning them down like a bug in a glass-covered display case.

All language, for Barthes, was like this. It collected clichés and fatuities as navels collect lint. The same old words forced the mind through the same old channels. And the repeat offender, the guiltiest culprit in this stacking of reality's cards, was the adjective. It was a chronic affliction of Barthes's own field, cultural criticism. Critics of ineffable arts like music and painting scrabbled around for adjectives when they had run out of better words. The laziest fell back on noisy superlatives, which were an admission of defeat in one's tug of war with language. These words were trying to describe something, such as a musical phrase, for which description would always fall short.

In his essay "African Grammar," Barthes explores the language used in French newspapers during the Algerian war of independence in the 1950s. The press defended the government's brutal suppression of the revolt by declaring that Algeria and France shared a common destiny and that the French still had a duty to rule over a less developed people. Barthes noted that the language favored abstract nouns over verbs, to suggest stability and permanence. But then, out of a fear that those nouns were tired, it paired them with reviving adjectives or adverbs. And so independence became *true*, aspirations *authentic* and destinies *indissolubly linked*. These extra words "cleared the noun of its past disappointments, presenting it in a new, innocent, credible state."

But this salvaging operation was doomed. The "adjectives of reinvigoration" were worn out as fast as they were used, to become instead "adjectives of essence." They no longer did the job of modifying the noun, because "independence cannot be anything but independent, friendship friendly, and cooperation unanimous." They could now only strive uselessly "to give nothingness the qualities of being."

•

Giving nothingness the qualities of being is a good summary of how not to use adjectives. Managerial blah is full of these hollow intensifiers, like *robust*, *proactive* or *strategic*, meant to assign macho purpose to the time-wasting and vacuous. Beware adjectives, too, that stick tautologically to nouns: *component parts*, *forward planning*, *personal belongings*. Or space-filling ones like *certain*, *various* and *any*, inconspicuous on their own but a choke on the writing when they accumulate.

Barthes is right. Writing about the ineffable does float thoughtlessly into the adjectival and end up smelling of neediness and unearned opinion. Book blurbs and reviewese are full of worn words like *high-octane*, *haunting* and *magisterial*, and adverb-adjective pairs like *searingly honest* or *stunningly accomplished*—phrases that sound odd when you say them aloud, because no one ever does.

A wine writer, trying to describe the evanescent impressions a certain vintage makes on the nose, palate and throat, must fall back on adjectives, or "descriptors" as they are known in the trade: *creamy, biscuity, peppery, toasty, plump*. Food writing uses less clichéd adjectives because food is more amenable to description. Food is not just its taste but its smell, warmth, chewiness, crispiness, crumbliness, juiciness and mushiness. It can also be underdone or burned. But wine is just taste and smell—or something vaguer than smell called *aroma*. To begin to describe it, you have to loot more description-friendly worlds for analogies and still it won't do. Wine-tasting notes are just flailing, adjective-addled impressions—like trying to paint a noise, or photograph a smell.

And yet Barthes's loathing of the adjective feels lopsided. Nouns are just as presumptuous as adjectives—perhaps more so, since a name is harder to disown than a description. In unreadable writing, adverbial or adjectival mildew is rarely the worst problem. (It can at least quickly be skimmed, while a misused preposition sinks the whole sentence.) Adverbs and adjectives get a bad rap because the good ones toil away, blameless and ignored. They turn up in the plainest prose, doing useful work. We notice them only when they are too much.

You cannot do without the adverbs that explain where something happens, like *nowhere* or *upstairs*, or when or how often, like *yesterday* or *more*. Adverbs simplify writing as well as embellish it. Latinate verbs can be swapped for those verb–adverb combos, common in English, called phrasal verbs. These replace one word with two (bad) but they use strong verbs and cut syllables (good). *Illuminate*: *light up*. *Extinguish*: *put out*. *Surrender*: *give up*.

When plain stylists call for the culling of adverbs, they mean one kind: those that add the suffix *-ly* to an adjective. But these account for less than a third of adverbs. If you cannot work out which part of speech a word is in a sentence—*first, back, away, well, not, never, abroad*—it is probably an adverb. Old English gives us many flat adverbs (ones that have the same form as their matching adjective) and they are often single-syllabled and avoid those dull -*ly* sounds.

Tyndale is sparing with adverbs. His *My soul is heavy even unto the death* reads better than the King James's *My soul is exceeding sorrowful even unto death* because the adverb *exceeding* waters down the thought. Likewise the *indeed* in the King James's *The spirit indeed is willing*, which Tyndale does without. But he uses flat adverbs as intensifiers quite freely. They were *sore* afraid. Is his mercy *clean* gone? I will awake *right* early. Flat adverbs add a sharp, stressed syllable to the end of a clause. Chop it up *small*. The moon shone *bright*. I did it *wrong*.

Adjectives can add precision to a sentence, too. Many have absolute meanings, which means they do not have comparative or superlative forms and cannot be intensified with adverbs. You cannot be *slightly married* or *very dead*. A *wooden* floor cannot be any more wooden than it already is, or woodier than the other wooden floors, or the woodenest. A squash ball is no more *spherical* than a billiard ball.

As for descriptive adjectives, they can be overcooked, but so what? Wine writing may be a fool's errand but that is wine's fault for making us foolish by tempting us to describe it—the joys it gives, the moods it stirs, the tastes it complements, the sorrows it drowns. To give up on describing the ineffable is a counsel of despair, a refusal of the effervescence of language. We will always want to expend our descriptive energies on the things that are, in the end, beyond the reach of words.

•

Note that, in the quotes above, Barthes uses adjectives: *new, innocent, credible*. And that when he calls the adjective "the poorest of linguistic categories," he needs two adjectives to do it. Adjectives, like weeds, cannot be eradicated, only tamed. Nor, as with weeds, should we always try to tame them. Gardeners hate weeds because they threaten the neat, humanized geometry of their gardens. But if you have no such narrow ideas of neatness, the irrepressibility of weeds is easy to admire. You can hack at them with a machete or murder them with chemicals and they just keep growing back. Weeds bespeak the anarchic profligacy of nature.

Adjectives have something of that same florid verve. Like weeds they are inherently untidy, sometimes ugly, always ungovernable. The plain stylist stigmatizes them as the gardener stigmatizes weeds, because they disturb his ideas of purity. And yet, just as a weed is only a plant growing in the wrong place, and one person's weed is another's wild beauty, so an adjective in the right place can be wildly beautiful.

An adjective should make a noun more specific, or vivid, or both. (The same goes for an adverb acting on a verb.) When Laurie Lee writes of his Cotswolds childhood that "we led marooned lives, marooned by nature and by lack of transport," that repeated participle is perfect. Participles, used as modifiers, always inject a shot of verbal energy: *running water, broken heart, lost soul, escaped lion.* Lee's *marooned* is also a transferred epithet, an adjective stuck to the "wrong" noun, as in *restless night* (the insomniac being the restless one, not the night) or *awkward silence* (the silent people being the awkward ones, not the silence). When adjectives transfer from human to nonhuman things like this, they imbue the abstract or inert with agency and purpose. A life cannot really be marooned. But *marooned* is just right, because it suggests both verbal energy and helplessness. The young Laurie Lee led a marooned life.

Often the biggest call to make about an adjective is not whether to use it but where to put it in the sentence. Dan Brown, author of *The Da Vinci Code*, is often mocked for his overeager adjectives like *famous* and *renowned*. If you have to describe someone as famous or renowned, then they are probably not famous or renowned enough. Trust me, these adjectives are saying, this thing merits your notice. See also *seminal, prestigious, significant, iconic* and *meaningful* ("usually a meaningless word"—Christopher Lasch). But a much bigger problem is that Brown likes to put his adjectives in just one place—before the noun. When every noun has a tagalong premodifier, it taps out trite rhythms, as in this sentence from *Inferno*: "He had a shaggy beard, bushy mustache, and gentle eyes that radiated a thoughtful calm beneath his overgrown eyebrows."

You can avoid these adjective-addled nouns by putting the adjective after the noun. An adjectival cluster at the end of a sentence colors in the noun after it has been sketched out. A dog on a lead is an explorer, *straining, slack-jawed, alert*. Move adjectives after the verb and they become the predicate, the main news of the sentence. Here, being more exposed, they are less likely to be filler. At the end of a sentence, with nowhere to hide, adjectives must be *enlarging* and *apropos*.

The aim, in the plain style as in all styles, is to make something disordered and random feel measured and deliberate. Choosing the right words is difficult, and our first efforts always sound gauche and try-too-hard. "What is style?" asks Barthes in an essay on sport. "Style makes a difficult action into a graceful gesture, introduces a rhythm into fatality. Style is to be courageous without disorder, to give necessity the appearance of freedom." Writing gives necessity the appearance of freedom when the words no longer look as if they are laboring to belong. For an adjective or adverb to belong, it must obey this iron law: the right word is only the right word in the right place.

•

Back we come, as ever, to syntax. What the plain stylists really mean by scorning adjectives and adverbs is that sentences come alive through word order, not strained effect. The plain style draws its power from the sequence of the words and the way that it drives the sentence onwards to its full stop. Needless intensifiers slow that journey down. Plain stylists dislike too much punctuation for the same reason: it delays this drive to the sentence's end. The quickest route between two points is a straight line.

The problem with punctuation is that no one can decide what it is for. It came into being as authors and printers tried to wrest interpretive authority away from readers. Ancient texts did not need even the most basic punctuation, word division. They were written in *scriptio continua*—words with no spaces in between. Marking out spaces would have meant taking the power of interpretation away from readers, who were the elite, and giving it to the scribes, who were slaves.

The monk-scribes of Ireland, writing out copies of the Bible to be read in church, were pioneers of punctuation. The early Christian Church recruited from all classes, not just the elite readers that classical texts had. These Irish clerics worried about how the Bible should be read aloud to the uneducated flock, where to leave punctuating pauses so that its "true" sense—the sense *they* gave it, of course—could be got. Irish is not a Romance language, so the Latin of the Vulgate Bible was unlike the language the monks spoke. This estranging aspect made them see it as a solely written language. Writing was coming to be seen less as a record of speech than as a thing in itself, hurrying straight to the mind through the eye. The monks abandoned *scriptio continua*, put spaces between words and added the graphic marks that became punctuation.

The first punctuation marks drew on the basic medieval form of musical notation, the *neume*, which comes from the Greek *pneuma*, for "breath." This early punctuation aided reading aloud, just as notation aided singing aloud, by telling the speaker when to breathe. Older texts tend to scatter commas and dashes like wedding rice, because they see them as pauses for breath—crucial because sentences were much longer then. Punctuation retains this sense of itself as a breathing pause, helping the reader turn the words into speech in her head. But now it has another role: to clarify syntax, marking phrasal divides and dispelling confusion in the solitude of silent reading.

In the first volume of his autobiography, Karl Ove Knausgaard describes the vertiginous feeling of reading Theodor Adorno as a young man. Every full stop of this difficult thinker's writings was "set like a mountaineer's cleat," he writes, in admiration and exasperation. It left Knausgaard feeling slightly oxygen-deprived and intoxicated by his own cleverness. Getting to the end of just one Adorno sentence was a small triumph.

In his essay "Punctuation Marks," Adorno claimed that these marks were where language most resembled music. Perhaps because he was also a composer, he heard sounds in them. Exclamation points were cymbal clashes, question marks musical upbeats, and colons dominant seventh chords. He feared that, in an age when readability was now the supreme value, the most nuanced mark, the semicolon, would die. The consumer's fear of page-long paragraphs—the kind Adorno liked to write—would reduce writing to a mere "protocol sentence." What started with the loss of the semicolon would end with "the ratification of imbecility by a reasonableness purged of all admixtures."

Ornate stylists see punctuation as Adorno does—as a sort of vivid musical notation, annotating the text to bring it to life. Plain stylists see punctuation instead as a necessary evil, to be resorted to only when the syntax will not do the job. Their ideal is to write a clear, longish sentence with no internal punctuation at all, not even a comma. They reserve a special animus for Adorno's favorite mark, the semicolon. Orwell dismissed it as an "unnecessary stop." Donald Barthelme thought it "ugly as a tick on a dog's belly." Samuel Beckett called it "hideous" in his novel *Watt* (albeit straight after using one and just before using another one). The poet Richard Hugo complained that "semicolons indicate relationships that only idiots need defined by punctuation."

The reason for their irritation, I think, is that the semicolon inserts a more subtle break than mere syntax or breathing pauses require. Other marks, like commas and dashes, reflect the natural stops of speech. But among punctuation marks the semicolon was a late bloomer, devised by Venetian printers only at the end of the fifteenth century. It came out of the search for a more finely attuned pause somewhere between the colon and the comma, in a new print culture in which writer and reader were strangers.

Unlike Orwell et al., I do not think of semicolons as just neurotic commas; I can see they have their uses. But sometimes they let you stretch out a sentence lazily, stuffing thoughts together without bothering to better order the words. Or they semi-rescue sentences that would be better off cut up or recast. Or they are quick fixes, ending a clause without you having to come up with a strong stress. Managerial blah uses semicolons to patch clauses together when the verbs are not strong enough to carry the reader through the sentence and into the next one. Colons are just as guilty: they, too, can patch up weak syntax with punctuating sticking plaster. They are artificially prolonging the life of a sentence that would be best left to die.

●

At one of her readings, the poet Mary Oliver joked, while introducing her punctuation-less poem "Seven White Butterflies," that every writer has a quota of punctuation. This finite amount must be spread thinly across a lifetime, she said, lest we suddenly hear a voice saying: "No more semicolons."

I like the idea of punctuation being rationed, like food and fuel in wartime. Writers could each be given a ration book, with a set number of coupons for each punctuation mark. Semicolons would be rationed as meanly as petrol, because most of us could do without them, just as we could do without a car if we had to. Commas would be more generously rationed, like tea or sugar—because these are not quite luxuries, but nor should we behave as if they were in bottomless supply. Only one punctuation mark would be off the ration, for without it no sentence can exist: the full stop.

The purest sentence in the plain style needs only a full stop. We must learn to love it above all other marks, and think of it as the goal toward which all words adamantly move. The full stop offers the reader a brief let-up, a sense that the point of that sentence is done and its meaning has been fulfilled. The Belgian-French poet Henri Michaux saw the finitude of our lives encapsulated in this "dot that death devours." We owe nature our deaths, said Freud, and the death of a sentence is as natural as the end of a life. Every sentence must die so the next one can begin. A full stop should offer a good death: natural, painless, clarifying, renewing.

The need for a semicolon is a matter of taste, but the need for a full stop is a matter of fact. You cannot write a sentence until you have mastered the bare bones of the full stop: why you need it, where to put it and what to put just before it. It is the writer's fail-safe and the reader's friend, the giver of clarity, rhythm and relief. It gives clarity because it turns the words that precede it into a self-sufficient whole. It gives rhythm because the full stops come in different places, cutting off short and long groups of words, varying the pace and the music. And it gives relief because it brings the thought to rest and takes a breath before the next one begins. All this needs to be said now more than ever, for we live in an age when the full stop is losing its power.

There is a sure way of spotting older computer users like me: we hit two spaces after each full stop. I did this for years before an editor told me how annoying it was. Typesetters hate it because it leads to runlets of white space coursing down the page, called *rivering*. This two-space habit outs you as someone who learned to type on a mechanical typewriter. Non-electric typewriters had monospaced fonts, with each letter taking up the same amount of space, which left a lot of space between letters, especially thin ones like *i* and *l*, and made it harder to spot the gaps between sentences, because they did not stand out. So two spaces at the start of a sentence marked a clean break and declared that you were starting afresh.

Monospacing also meant that the typewriter's full stop was a large black blob, as wide as a letter. When electric typewriters, and then word processors, brought in typefaces with proportional spacing, the full stop became a small dot that did not require two spaces after it. The effect, at least as it seemed to this ex-typewriter user, was to make the full stop matter less. On a typewriter the full stop was a prominent key, second from the right after the shift key on the bottom row. On a keyboard it was more discreet, sitting alongside function keys with odd-looking icons and abbreviations, the point of which I still haven't worked out after thirty years of computing. The most crucial part of the sentence became a mere speck: easy to miss, easy to insert as an afterthought.

•

Then came another threat to the full stop: the talky, casual prose of texting and online chat. The dialogic visual language of texting speech bubbles, pinging left and right on your phone, has little use for full stops. A single-line text needs no punctuation to show that it has ended. Instead of a full stop we press send. Longer texts replace the full stop with a simple line break, which has assumed the role of an all-purpose, pause-inserting mark, like the medieval *punctus*. The ends of these texts are marked by three-dot ellipses, kisses or emojis.

Omitting the full stop gives off an extempore air, making replies seem insouciant and jokes unrehearsed. Studies have shown that young people tend to read a full stop in a text as clipped, curt or passive-aggressive. On social media, they use full stops between every word to sound angrily emphatic. *End. Of. Story.* But a full stop is not meant to be the final word in an argument. It is a satisfying little click that moves the dial along so the next sentence can pick up where it left off. Its end is also a beginning.

More people than ever are writing sentences. In the 1960s Marshall McLuhan speculated that technology would one day allow us to communicate our perceptions direct, without the flawed medium of writing. A Catholic convert, he thought that new media might create a "unified sensorium" and "a general cosmic consciousness." He believed that the computer could bring about a global Pentecost, a revelation of the Holy Spirit without the evasions of language. In the future we would commune our thoughts intuitively like St. Augustine's angels, unmediated by words.

A more modest variant on this article of faith is the belief that voice recognition will do away with keyboards. Writing is an arduous and energy-consuming act: why bother with it when you could use something as easy and natural as a voice? In a 2002 *Harper's* essay, Marshall Fisher claimed that typing would soon survive as just a sense memory. "A writer," he wrote, "while composing with his voice, will still tap his fingers on the desk like an amputee scratching a wooden leg."

The opposite occurred. Far from writing being replaced by mind-melding or dictation to electronic secretaries, it has flourished. If you time-traveled even just thirty years back, you would be struck by how little writing was happening, outside of the classroom or lecture hall. No customers sat in coffee chains stabbing their laptops urgently with two fingers. No students texting slyly in class under their desks. No one updating the social network with the headline news of their lives. You might see the odd soul scrawling a signature on a checkbook or a new appointment in their Filofax. But mostly writing would have been farmed out to the professionals.

Little did they know that they were living at the end of days. They were the last generation in a long era—let's call it the *printocene*—when writing was meant to be read much later than it was written. Nowadays most writing is for rapid release and response, a slightly interrupted way of having a conversation.

We live in an age that overprizes speech—that likes to pretend that writing *is* speech. All over the world people are writing, tapping out e-mails or texting friends with that familiar, two-thumb dance. It happens everywhere from commuter trains to marital beds. We write in the places where we talk and as if we were talking, somehow managing to tune out the hum of a hundred other conversations going on simultaneously. We are all writing and talking over the top of each other.

•

Some sentences fail because they don't sing in our heads; they have moved too far from the rhythm and kinesis of speech. But unpunctuated text-speak fails for the opposite reason. It wants so much to be like speech that it has forgotten it is writing. It gestures toward its reader on an emotional level, just as people do when they say *know what I mean?*, but then forget to leave a pause for their listener to dissent.

Writing is not conversation, nor a speech-balloon text waiting for a response. The point of writing is to store and spread information in a form that does not require anyone else's bodily presence while it is being written. A sentence gives words a finished form that awaits no clarification. It is its own small island of sense, from which the writer has been airlifted and on which no one else need live. We write alone, as an act of faith in the power of words to speak to others who are unknown and elsewhere.

Hence the full stop. A sentence with a full stop needs no answering call, and rarely receives it. Writing's effects are hidden and circuitous, with none of the immediacy of speech. Speech is the vibration of that very stuff of life, air, as it moves up from the abdomen to the lips. A voice is a breathing body, the audible proof that a human being is alive at that moment, trying to make itself heard. A beautiful voice can soothe and bewitch the hearer in ways that inked words can't. Speak in a sonorous way and you change the weather in a room.

In Homer, characters address each other in *epea pteroenta*, or "wingèd words." These words fly between bodies and pierce the listener. Another translation is "feathered words"—feathered not like birds but like arrows, the feathers helping them to fly straight as a dart to their target. Words gather into meaning in the breast, impatient to come out, then escape from the teeth's enclosure like birds from a cage, or like feathered arrows from a bow, and fly into the ears of others. Wingèd words ensorcell the hearer and turn the speaker, if only for a moment, into a god.

When you write a sentence, nothing like that happens. In fact, nothing happens at all. Adding to the vast pile of existing sentences is like adding another stone to a hilltop cairn. You have agreed to join in one of humanity's joint endeavors—cairn-building or sentence-writing—when no one else is watching. The act is its own reward; do not expect applause. You must be willing to keep writing in the absence of any evidence that anyone is reading. And no use complaining either, since no one asked you to do it in the first place. The rewards of writing sentences are real, but they are long-deferred and mostly unconfirmed.

Writing should have an air of address, a sense of being aimed at someone, albeit not like an arrow. One way to invoke such a quasi-dialogue is to end the odd sentence with a question mark. This shifts the center of gravity toward the reader, even if the writer is just asking and then answering her own questions. Overdone, though, it reads like a tic, rather like that rising inflection, or Australian upspeak, at the end of a spoken phrase. A sentence should assume the reader's existence but cannot keep demanding a response. So it needs a full stop to end the thought, like a life needs an end.

•

With a full stop, a sentence becomes self-supporting. It can go out into the world without the author leaning over the reader to clarify its meaning—without a reader, even, except a conjectural one. Writing a sentence well involves caring, taking pains for the benefit of others. But it is a special kind of caring: not the empathetic concern we have for people we love, but care for the anonymous humanity that may, at some future point, encounter the evidence of our presence in the world. This kind of care does not seek thanks or feedback, but offers itself up for all to enjoy, or ignore, as they wish.

Without these no-strings acts that stand uncoupled from their makers, society could not work and life would not be worth living. A town square, a city park or a public footpath communicate that kind of care. These things are just there for all to use, soundlessly speaking to our shared humanity and the life we have in common. A well-made sentence shows the same silent solicitude for others. It cares.

The cathedral across the road from me cares in this way. It welcomes all, believers and heathens alike, giving them no orders or instructions on how to use it. So they end up using it in unusual ways. On the piazza built over the roof of the crypt, impromptu games of football break out. On the outdoor plinths, lunches are unpacked and eaten. On the steps up to the entrance, the same man jogs eternally up and down, like Rocky Balboa on the steps of the Philadelphia Museum of Art. The cathedral invites you in without requiring faith or commitment, or asking you, with jazz-hands brightness, to *get involved* or *have your say*. When the rest of the world feels shouty and oversold, I go there and sit with myself for a while. For here is somewhere that asks only that I match its quietness with my own.

We need spaces like this, that feel solid and anchoring and that care for us in unspoken, undemanding ways. We need sentences like this, too. The restraint of the full stop, and the little pause it interposes, feels even more precious in our age of over-sharing and emotional unrestraint. In the care of a cathedral, or a sentence, we feel as if a little alcove of sense and order has been carved out in our minds, before we are decanted once again into the noise and haste of our lives.

∙

In April 1972 the film star George Sanders checked into a hotel room in a seaside town near Barcelona and took five bottles of Nembutal. He left behind a note containing four pellucid sentences. *Dear World: I am leaving because I am bored. I feel I have lived long enough. I am leaving you with your worries in this sweet cesspool. Good luck.* In under thirty words, Sanders managed to sound like an authentic voice speaking to an audience. His full stops were as clean as bullet holes.

It might seem odd to think of a suicide note as showing the same kind of care for others as a cathedral. But, in one narrow sense, Sanders's note did. Like a message in a bottle flung into the sea, it was unsullied by any demand for a response from its reader. One might say that every successful piece of writing begins "Dear World," even if the words are only implied. Sanders's life was a mess at its end. His film career was over, he was broke, his fourth marriage had lasted eight weeks, he was drinking heavily and his health was poor. But his suicide note was as impeccable as his film persona—elegantly mannered, smoothly cynical and, in its own way, generous.

Sentence writers are not negotiating with their readers. They are benign dictators delivering *faits accomplis*. They must instruct themselves and decide on their own that the sentence has arrived at its end. Skilled writers have read and absorbed lots of proofread, published sentences, not just the unrefined ones we send to each other online. And when they set down a sentence, these other sentences play very quietly in their heads. What do these sentences have in common, and what makes them cleave to the reader's cerebral cortex and pulsate with life?

Their full stops, arriving in the right place and, together, making music.

•

A plain English sentence moves smoothly and easily toward its final point. The best way to ensure this happens is to put the important stuff at the end. A sentence ordered like this feels more deliberate and more memorable, just as, when you stop speaking, what stays in your listener's mind is the last thing you said. A sentence's strongest stress falls on its last stressed syllable. Thus a light, unstressed word like *to* or *of* may end a sentence tamely. A sentence has a special snap if its last syllable is stressed— a good way to end a paragraph, especially a final one. A short word will do the trick, and even better if it ends with a hard consonant that stops the breath and brings the voice to rest. *I binned that brainless book.*

The words at the end of a sentence are usually the predicate: the main verb and its complements. The predicate adds new information that the next sentence may then begin with as a given. Weak sentences break this given-then-new rule. The subject is stronger than the predicate, so the sentence ends with an unresounding *phhtt*. If you say that something is *an interesting factor to consider* or *should be borne in mind* or *is increasingly relevant in our globalized society*, then your predicate is just mumbly noise, because those things could be said not about something but about anything.

As Orwell noted in his essay "Politics and the English Language," these off-the-shelf phrases seduce writers because they are "more or less euphonious." They flesh out the sentence with harmless-sounding syllables and save it from crashing headlong into the full stop. Occasionally sentences with weak predicates achieve an air of euphoric understatement, like the one with which Francis Crick and James Watson announced their discovery of DNA's double helix in the journal *Nature*: "This structure has novel features which are of considerable biological interest." That predicate is so coy, so inadequate to the article's momentous findings, that it almost swaggers. Mostly, though, weak predicates are just weak. They feel like they should be the important bit of the sentence because they come at the end, but they sag under a weight they cannot hold.

I have written a few of these pretending-to-care sentences in my time. Such-and-such a thing was *deeply problematic* or *more crucial than ever before* or *a debate that is long overdue.* I blame the flawed premise of the academic essay, which is that the writer must pretend to care. The existentialists called this "bad faith," when we adopt social roles alien to our natures because we kid ourselves that we have no choice. As Jean-Paul Sartre wrote *Being and Nothingness* in a window seat in the Café de Flore in Paris, he was served by a surly waiter, whom he came to embody in the book as an archetype of such bad faith. This waiter, he fancied, was surly because he wanted to be an actor or an artist. He had to play the bourgeois game of pretending that waiting was all he wanted to do. His scowl gave him away.

My lame sentence endings were like that Parisian waiter, trying and failing to wear a convincing mask. I was adding words to make the sentence longer, bulking it out with platitude, playing the game—the one that tells you to pretend to care about the answer to someone else's question, and to come up with a fixed number of words in response to this set task. And, like the waiter, I had been rumbled. *An essay is an exercise in what Sartre calls "bad faith." Discuss.* A sentence brought properly to rest, with a full stop in the right place, says that its maker cared how its words fell on the reader's ear. The sentence feels fated to end thus, not just strung out to fill the word count.

•

Orwell saw the plain style as the sword of existential truth, a cure-all for the bad faith of modern life. But the myth of the plain style is that it is all about truth. The truth of the plain style is that it is all about skill. Here are some things Orwell told us with his plainclothes sentences. At prep school he was beaten with a riding crop for wetting the bed, and beaten so severely that the crop broke. Serving in the Burmese police, he shot an elephant that had run amok. Leaving Wigan by train, he saw through the window a woman poking a stick up a fetid drainpipe, and exchanged dark looks with her about her desperate life. Orwell's biographers have since shed doubt on all these stories. But the right words in the right order sound true. Skilled writers fit words together in a way that suggests a veracity and acuity they may themselves be far from possessing. Hugh Kenner wrote of the plain style that "nothing beats it as a vehicle for profitable lies."

Orwell's prose, as well as ignoring his own writing rules when it suits, is a beautiful contrivance. The last thing he wrote, in his hospital notebook, was this: "At 50, everyone has the face he deserves." This unforgettable sentence has an argument behind it that a moment's thought will reveal as unfair and untrue. Orwell's oeuvre is full of such sentences that read like eternal verities and turn out to be nonsense. "We may find in the long run that tinned food is a deadlier weapon than the machine gun." (We didn't.) "Serious sport ... is war minus the shooting." (War minus the shooting isn't war.) "Writing a book is a horrible, exhausting struggle, like a long bout of some painful illness." (Steady on.)

Orwell wrote in support of many causes and attitudes: the preservation of the traditional English pub, his dislike of park railings and "keep off the grass" busybodies, his hatred of sandal-wearing vegetarians, and his passionate conviction that, when making a cup of tea, the milk should be added last. But really he believed only in sentences—which, since he was a writer, is probably as it should be.

William Gass writes that the only people who treat the sentence with the seriousness it demands are "the liars who want to be believed." Novelists and poets know that all that matters is the words, that there is no reality apart from "the sounding syllables which the reader will speak into his own weary and distracted head." Does this mean you can write anything and declare it true? No. It means you have to search for the truth *in* your sentences, not outside of them. You have to give up all your pet ideas and idle prejudices and let the sentence tell you what you did not mean to say and may not wish to hear. The words and their order will do the work.

True is not just an adjective; it is a verb, meaning to prove or to make something true. Carpenters and engineers call it *trueing* or *trueing up*: making an object straight or level to the exact degree needed to fit its purpose. *We still have to true up the end face on the cylinder*, they say. The plain style is the writing equivalent of trueing up. It makes something true by making it look true.

•

Once you see this, you see that plain English can be used to say things that are far from plain. Learn to write in the plain style and you may be faithful to the oddness of the world. The world Tyndale rendered with plain words feels real but full of wonder. In the Vale of Berkeley, the flat lands by the Severn where he grew up, people spent their lives raising sheep, shearing them, washing the wool in streams, spinning yarn, weaving cloth and dyeing it. It was the same simple, pastoral life out of which the Bible harvests its metaphors—about sowing seeds, toiling in vineyards, losing sheep and longing for green pastures.

Much of the Bible happens outdoors, in deserts, mountains, rivers and fields. Here fearsome extremes—storms, floods, severe cold and intense heat—are part of daily life. God's people look with awe on clouds as the giver of rain for crops and imagine that God dwells in them. They see the grass wither swiftly after the seasonal rains and make it a symbol for the brevity of life.

Outdoors, life itself feels like a miracle. So when Balaam's ass starts to speak, or Jesus kills a fig tree with a curse, it can be put in the same plain sentences and still make perfect sense. The plain style embraces it all: daily bread and the Holy Ghost, hailstorms and locust plagues, the miracle of the sun rising each day and the miracle of Lazarus rising from the dead. It gives gravitas to the mundane and lightness to the grave. It renders the everyday astonishing and the astonishing everyday.

Tyndale uses plain words to say peculiar things. His Bible brims with sentences that are as simple in syntax as they are strange in sense, that start out plainly and then end in unexpected ways. *The kingdom of heaven is like unto ... a grain of mustard-seed. Hypocrite, first cast out ... the beam out of thine own eye. For we are ... a gazing stock unto the world.* When a sentence's content fights with its form, form wins, every time. Form tames the outlandish and makes it real, imposing a logic on the weirdness of the world. The plain style's power rests on this tension between the ease of its phrasing and the shock of its thought slid cleanly into the mind.

Tyndale's prose is not so much clear as memorable, and memorability is worth more in a sentence even than clarity. Or rather it is the best kind of clarity. The plain English style is just words worked into memorable forms that we define, post hoc, as clear, because they stay in our heads long enough to be understood. The lesson of all this is plain. If you have something weird or astonishing or heterodox to say—if you want to stretch the confines of the credible and be true to the world in all its beautiful, brain-melting absurdity, which you *should* want to do—then say it with the plainest words and in the plainest order you can find.

5.

The High-wire Act

Or how to write long and legato without running out of breath

Toward the end of the Second World War, a graduate student at Columbia University, Rudolf Flesch, began to think about what made so many English sentences so hard to read. Flesch, an Austrian refugee from the Nazis, approached the task with the uncluttered mind of a non-native speaker. According to the federal census, he noted, America now had 70,000 professional writers, more than it had shoemakers or fishermen. Most of them were not writing novels, but advice about how to fill in a tax return or wire a plug. Much of this writing, Flesch felt, was "gobbledygook"—a word he claimed to have invented. (The *OED* disagrees.)

Flesch thought that writing was a simple skill that we complicated uselessly. Most college composition courses confused students by getting them to diagram sentences in intricate ways—rather like starting a cookery course with bouillabaisse and crêpes Suzette. For Flesch, the secret of clear writing was to imitate speech. People understood each other when speaking because the listener could frown, look blank or prop up a sagging head with a hand if he was baffled or bored. (Not every speaker picks up on these cues, of course.) But a writer is talking to a reader who cannot talk back—who cannot even offer the basic feedback of screwing up his face and walking away. A bemused reader reproves the writer only with his invisible apathy. The reader has no voice, or not one that can be heard. All he can do is stop reading.

•

We must keep remembering, since we keep forgetting, that our writing will be read in our absence and it must clear up any confusion all on its own. Flesch felt that the best way to do this was to keep sentences short. Short sentences meant more full stops, which meant more breathing pauses and less chance of mangling the sense. He advised writers to keep sentences under twenty-five words. His golden mean was seventeen words, the average sentence length in *Reader's Digest*.

Flesch also recommended using short words. Long words, if they must be used, should be compound rather than complex. Compound words like *teapot* are easy for the reader to decipher because they split into two short words. Complex words are formed by adding an affix to a root word, so that *sign* becomes *signify* and then *signification*. These words take more mental effort to unpack. Flesch suggested swapping them for their root forms, or at least words with fewer affixes. "Talk about people in short sentences with many root words," he advised.

Flesch invented a formula for counting words and syllables in sentences and giving a piece of writing a "reading ease" score, from zero (unreadable) to one hundred (as easy as could be). Another readability expert, Robert P. Gunning, devised a rival scoring system, the fog index. To work out how forbidding a piece of writing is—how soupy its fog—you add the average number of words in a sentence to the average number of words of three or more syllables, and times it by point four. Writing with a fog rating of six can be navigated by a child; writing with a rating of sixteen needs a college graduate to get through it.

A new career was born: readability consultancy. Gunning's company, Readability Associates, taught the fog-count system to firms like Ford and American Airlines. Gunning and his assistants would descend like a team of troubleshooters and undertake a readability audit of the firm's literature, from minutes of meetings to office memos. For General Motors, Gunning made a Reading Ease calculator, a celluloid card and dial that worked like a slide rule to measure the clarity of prose. Readability was now an algorithm and it found much of writing wanting.

The Associated Press hired Flesch as a consultant, and the United Press hired Gunning. American newspapers at this time liked to open stories with a single, massive, summarizing sentence, a practice dating back to the civil war. While reporters were sending stories from the battlefields, the Morse telegraph would often break down. So they started hanging all the important stuff in an opening, one-sentence paragraph, the "clothesline lead," and the habit stuck. Flesch and Gunning tried, without much success, to get journalists to shorten their sentences.

Almost all writers make this mistake: stuffing too much into one sentence. At its root is the same old problem of having too much to say and thinking that the reader will be as fascinated in it as we are. We forget that writing is not about telling all, sweeping up the contents of the world and emptying them into the refuse bin of a sentence, but about withholding and releasing what we have to say bit by bit, because sentences can only be read bit by bit. For some reason we ignore the solution staring back at us: add a full stop and start again.

Readability is a misnomer. All writing that is not gibberish is readable, because it can be read. If someone is interested enough in the subject, they will stumble through the foggiest prose. Classical scholars will bother to crack hieroglyphics or Linear B, and all scholars will read unappetizing prose by their peers on topics that fascinate them. When the audience is as captive as this, the writing tends to deteriorate, but it is still, literally, readable. All *readable* means is that the writing goes down well, in the same way that a wine is called *drinkable* or a person *likable* (when surely these are minimum requirements).

For most writing, readability exerts a healthy market pressure. Gunning found that *Harper's* and *Atlantic Monthly* were read mostly by college graduates, but the writing in them averaged a fog rating at high-school level. The least readable magazine was *Playboy*, leading Gunning to ascribe its sales to "some factor other than writing style." He found that magazine editors wrote foggier sentences than those of the writers they hired. As writers they spoiled themselves with big words; as readers they were less indulgent.

"Write unto others as you would be written to" is a sensible rule, but hard to live by, because the reader in us is riven from the writer. Happily, though, this means that even people who write unreadable sentences prefer to read readable ones. Those who write clearly are repaid with the attention of others, including those who cannot write clearly at all.

•

Sentences are getting shorter. At the start of the seventeenth century, the first great age of English prose writing, the average length of a sentence was forty-five words. This length held steady in the eighteenth century and then began to fall. In the nineteenth century it was in the thirties; now it is in the twenties. The English sentence, besieged by short writing from the fragments of ad copy to character-limited tweets, has shed words and narrowed the gap between full stops. The great sentence shortening of the last 200 years is probably ongoing.

In the 1980s the early word-processing programs began to include reading-ease scores. Readability was now outsourced to electronic algorithms that could spot overlong sentences in seconds and find them guilty of fog. American insurance policies and safety manuals began aiming for a Flesch reading age of thirteen, the average among adults. Some government websites pledged never to publish a sentence of more than twenty-five words.

This all makes readability seem both complex, because it involves very hard sums, and simple, because it can be reduced to a precise-looking score, down to a fourth decimal place. Ours is the age of the algorithm. We believe that if we can just work out all the variables, we can design a model that ensures consistent performance. A paradigm of postwar corporate life, in fact: a complex formula that stops us having to think.

Perhaps I shouldn't be so dismissive. An app can beat me at chess, and thrash me at Scrabble even at entry level. Why would it not be able to best me at writing a sentence? All writing is algorithmic in part. Dean Hachamovitch, who invented Microsoft Word's autocorrect function, ascribed its success to the fact that typing is "a little bit of creativity and a whole lot of scut work." Autocorrect capitalizes the first word of a sentence, weeds out accidental double capitals, hoovers up typos, like the common *teh* for *the*, and even completes long words. None of this writes the sentence for you, but it helps.

The new neural network computers do more than autocorrect words: they finish sentences that you have started to write. This sentence-building software has been driven by touchscreen typing on mobiles and tablets. Our stubby little fingers land badly on virtual keyboards and need help to fix their mistakes. The software can be fed thousands of books, which it keeps in datasets that serve as storage containers for the contents of future sentences. Mills & Boon novels are preferred because their syntax is simple and copyable.

A neural network mimics the human brain, "learning" by shoring up neural pathways and building wisdom over time. Having seen the sentence *Let's meet at the airport*, it can infer that *office* or *hotel* could take the place of *airport*, and also that *Let's meet at the airport* has a similar shape to *Let's eat in the garden*. A neural network can turn raw data into a news report, compose a tweet that sounds like a person, even put together a passable sonnet.

So perhaps it is just that the algorithms are not clever enough yet. How about a program that spotted you were using *is* too much, and proposed stronger verbs? Or that told you how varied your sentences were in length, and then suggested ways of splitting up the longer ones? Or that said: Are you *sure* you want to use the word *simply* again? (A bad habit of mine.) Much of writing is scut work, and much of rewriting is making our pat phrases and lazy repetitions visible. Algorithms help. By routinizing the mundane tasks, they free the mind to focus on those elusive parts of writing that cannot be done algorithmically.

But those elusive parts are everything. A sentence written solely via some slide-rule calculus of readability will never be quite good enough. Writing has to be humanly messy, nonalgorithmically flawed, to be truly readable. Something in us balks at the idea of applying algebra to words, because words, unlike numbers, can move, hurt, anger, enchant and cajole, and build credible worlds of thought and feeling out of nothing. That "little bit of creativity" is all. A sentence needs a glint of human intelligence behind it to give it the elusive thing, sentience, that makes it a sentence.

•

On one point the readability research is irrefutable. As average sentence length rises, comprehension falls. Chains of long sentences with long words are off-putting to even the most able reader. After about twenty-five words, a sentence is getting into its third clause, or maybe the second phrase after a main clause. The reader's memory starts to crumple under the weight. From about the age of nine, our eyes bounce around the page, reading only about a quarter of the words. Long sentences are harder to skim and need more working memory to get through them. So they are harder to read—or harder to write in a way that is easy to read. A reader needs a reason to schlepp through a long sentence.

There is a judge on a baking competition I watch on television who says that a poorly baked cake is "not worth the calories." I am not sure I agree. A poorly baked cake is still cake, after all. But applied to writing, this kind of trade-off makes sense. Long sentences need to justify the mental labor spent on them. Few turn out to be worth the words.

I learned this lesson late. For years I thought it was enough to use strong syntax and words that were not deliberately abstruse. I did not see that if you routinely use common but longer words—*phenomenon*, not *thing*; *approximately*, not *about*; *superior*, not *better*; *utilize*, not *use*—you are adding to the syllables that the reader has to read. All the words can be understood, and the word order is clear, and yet the sentence is still a slog.

I had also thought that complex ideas needed complex sentences. But when the ideas are complex, it is even more crucial not to saddle the reader with long words and phrases, so he can expend his mental energy on the ideas. The sentences of "difficult" writers like Nietzsche, Kafka and Beckett are often as short and clear as those in Mr. Men books. They may be hard to fathom but they are seldom hard to read. No evidence exists, however comforting its discovery might be for those of us who find it difficult to be easy, that difficulty in writing is a mark of profundity. More likely, long sentences are just overgrown graveyards where unconvincing arguments are conveniently buried.

On something else, though, readability research is clear: there is nothing wrong with long sentences per se. Average sentence length, not some arbitrary maximum, is what counts. Long sentences and long words are fine so long as they bump up against short ones. They are the symptoms of fog, not their cause. A style doctor diagnosing the disease of bad sentences might see length as a worrying sign, but then find that the roots of unreadability lie elsewhere. A bad sentence is made worse by being longer, but it was bad to begin with.

•

Long sentences have their uses. They can be more concise than a string of simple ones, because having a subject and main verb for each thought wastes words. And sometimes long sentences are useful for the opposite reason: not to save words but to expend them, to stretch out a thought so the reader can keep up as you think it through. "To know that simplifying may often mean expanding," Flesch wrote, "is the beginning of wisdom."

Flesch thought that the secret of plain language was "inbetween space." When we talk to someone, our pauses and recaps give our listener space to process the message. Clear writing, too, is "heavy stuff packed with excelsior." Excelsior was the American trade name for the curled wood shavings used to pack fragile items and stuff furniture. Flesch thought that plain writing, like plain talk, used these wood-shaving words as a thought cushion between the heavy stuff.

Of course this goes against the plain-style orthodoxy: *If you can cut a word, do.* The orthodoxy is right, but not every time. A sentence should use no more words than it needs, but working out what *needs* means is not straightforward. Mostly, writing should edit out the redundancies of speech. But if every word feels equally vital, the sentence is firing too much information too quickly at the reader and he cannot absorb it all.

Linguists distinguish between content and non-content words. The content words are the nouns, verbs, adjectives and adverbs that bear the main load of meaning. The non-content words are the little words, like prepositions, articles, pronouns and conjunctions, that glue the sentence together. This difference gives an English sentence its rhythm, because, when we read it aloud or sound it in our heads, we stress the content words and skate lightly over the non-content ones. I *dropped* my *phone* down the *toilet* and *watched* it *vanish* up the *U-bend*.

Speech is more intricate in its syntax than writing. It has shorter clauses and more non-content words to link these clauses up. Writing is denser, with longer clauses and more content words. Speech is simple words in complex sentences; writing is complex words in simple sentences. "The complexity of speech is choreographic—an intricacy of movement," the linguist Michael Halliday writes. "That of writing is crystalline—a denseness of matter." Academic writing is especially dense. It is often accused of being wordy, but that is not quite right. It may use big words, but the sentences they appear in are an impacted mass with few words wasted.

These kinds of sentences can be made more readable by cutting deadwood words *and* adding words. By expanding complex ideas into long, loose sentences, you mimic the stretched-out thinking-aloudness of speech. Cutting out long, derived words, such as nominalizations, often means using more words in their place—but it can make the writing feel less squashed. The slow train of thought needs plenty of track.

This way of making a long sentence clearer sounds counter-intuitive: make the sentence even longer by using more words. But the extra words help because they mark the start of phrases, so they break the sentence up into readable little chunks. Take this famous sentence from the autobiography of the historian George Macaulay Trevelyan: "The poetry of history lies in the quasi-miraculous fact that once, on this earth, once, on this familiar spot of ground, walked other men and women, as actual as we are today, thinking their own thoughts, swayed by their own passions, but now all gone, one generation vanishing into another, gone as utterly as we ourselves shall shortly be gone, like ghosts at cockcrow."

Trevelyan did not need to repeat *once* or *gone* there. But those words put a marker down at the start or end of phrases, making it easier for the reader to unstitch it all. The phrases are of similar shape and length and can be said, or heard in the head, as those trusty two-second intonation units. The sentence is sixty-four words long and slips down like a clam without touching the sides.

Being sparing with words does not mean being miserly with them. Words are there to be spent. Even a seemingly redundant word can add a euphonious beat, or give the reader time to think, or parcel out the sense better, or just make the sentence seem as if it comes from a real, human voice. Economy in writing is a virtue but it can be overprized. Sentences need some elbow room to move around in. "Writing is not an exercise in excision, it's a journey into sound," wrote E. B. White to a reader who was too slavishly following that famous advice from Strunk and White's *The Elements of Style*: "Omit needless words."

•

Sometimes sentences just need to be long. The world resists our efforts to enclose it between a capital and a full stop. Why, Malcolm Bowie asks, does Proust write such long, vermiform sentences, always subdividing then reassembling, loath to come to rest? Because, he says, they mimic the workings of desire and the neurotic rereading of situations we make when we are in love. Their denial and shaky restoration of meaning is "Eros become visible." Such sentences are like "all speculation, all mental efforts to make headway, in a resistant medium, toward a desired goal." They withhold their end because life is like that, refusing to fold itself neatly into subject, verb and object.

A long sentence should exult in its own expansiveness, lovingly extending its line of thought while being always clearly moving to its close. It should create anticipation, not confusion, as it goes along. The hard part is telling the difference between the two. I once heard Ken Dodd say that the secret of a great comedian is that he makes the audience feel simultaneously safe and slightly on edge. He has about half a minute from coming on stage, Dodd reckoned, to establish that he is harmless. He must quickly convey calm and control, so that the audience members relax into their seats, safe in the knowledge that nothing truly awkward is about to happen. But he must also create a sense of unpredictability that makes them lean forward. A good sentence has that same tension. It should frustrate readers just a little, and put them just faintly on edge, without ever suggesting that it has lost command of what is being said.

A sentence, once begun, demands its own completion. It throws a thought into the air and leaves the reader vaguely dissatisfied until that thought has come in to land. We read a sentence with the same part of our brains that processes music. Like music, a sentence arrays its elements into an order that should seem fresh and surprising and yet shaped and controlled. It works by violating expectations and creating mild frustrations on the way to fulfillment. As it runs its course, it assuages some of the frustration and may create more. But by the end, things should have resolved themselves in a way that allows something, at least, to be said.

•

A long sentence can seem thrillingly out of breath, deliciously tantalizing, so long as we feel the writer is still in charge. It is like listening to a great singer as he holds his breath and prolongs a phrase. The secret to Frank Sinatra's singing is his gift for fluid phrasing. Matt Monro may have had better technique, Tony Bennett more lung power, Nat King Cole a smoother tone, Bobby Darin more swing. But Sinatra beat them all at breathing.

As a young singer, Sinatra listened awestruck to his bandleader Tommy Dorsey's astoundingly smooth trombone playing. The note holds seemed to defy human lung capacity. Dorsey would play a musical phrase right through, seemingly without taking a breath, for eight or even sixteen bars. Sinatra sat behind him on the bandstand to learn when and how he breathed, but could not even see his jacket move up and down. Eventually he worked out that Dorsey had a pinhole in the corner of his mouth through which he was taking furtive breaths. Sinatra came to see that singing, too, was about breath control and that the secret was never to break the phrase. In music, *legato* means "bound together": a seamless flow, with no break between the notes. Sinatra wanted to sing legato, running the whole phrase into one smooth breath.

He worked out on running tracks and practiced holding his breath underwater in public pools, thinking song lyrics to himself as he swam. His breath control got better and, where he had to breathe in a song, he got better at hiding it. He moved the microphone toward and away from his mouth as he sang so that you never heard him inhale. If he had to sneak in a little breath somewhere he made sure it seemed deliberate, as if he were letting the message sink in. He learned this trick from watching the horn section in Dorsey's band during long instrumentals. When he sang, it sounded as if he was making it all up as he went along, pausing to pluck a word out of the air, lagging a fraction behind the beat—like a long, lithe sentence, *ad libitum* but always in control of what it was saying.

Unlike writing, which runs with its own irregular pulse, music has a regular rhythm with a steady downbeat. Musical meter controls time completely: a half note hangs in the air for exactly half as long as the whole note. This allows harmonizing singers and instruments to pursue separate agendas and yet still pleasurably coincide. But music also depends on phrasing, which is more subtle and varied than meter. A musical phrase lasts for about as long as a person can sing, or blow a wind instrument, in a single breath. What phrasing does to music is more like what a sentence does to words. A skilled singer can make the phrasing, the sentence structure of a song, work with or against the meter.

Pub crooners and karaoke singers never sing in sentences. They focus too much on lung power and hitting the notes and not enough on the words. They just belt it all out, taking gulping breaths midline, killing the meaning and the mood. But skilled singers know that the words matter. They might hold a note for effect, or add a bit of melisma, but mostly their phrasing will mirror the way the words of the song would be spoken. Songs are written in sentences, and phrasing is about singing in sentences, not song lines.

A phraseologist like Sinatra overlays the meter with something like confiding speech. He is all about the lyrics—you can hear him enunciate every syllable—and it feels as if he is saying as well as singing them to you, stretching out and twisting the pitch of words as we do in speech. Sinatra sings in sentences. Perhaps he hated rock 'n' roll for this reason, not because he thought it ugly and degenerate, as he said, but because it did not care about the sentences. The rhythm of rock 'n' roll always drowns out the syntax. Even a great phrasemaker like Chuck Berry has to make his sentences fit the backbeat.

It always irked me that in record shops Sinatra was filed under "easy listening," the suggestion being that his songs were as undemanding as elevator music, and best heard as the background buzz in a cocktail lounge. Another unfashionable singer filed in the same section, and whom I unfashionably loved, was Karen Carpenter. The emotional power of Carpenter's singing comes not so much from her vocal tone, gorgeous as that is, but from the fact that she, like Sinatra, sings in sentences. Singing for as long as she does on one breath, in complete sentences over twisting melodies, is an amazing feat—not just of lung capacity but of tricking her throat into thinking that she is not about to swallow.

By the end of a Carpenters song you feel wrung out, as if someone has emptied their heart in front of you. All that has happened is that you have been sucker punched by the dexterity of a technical virtuoso, effortlessly unspooling a long sentence. Easy listening is hard singing—and easy reading is hard writing.

•

How do you write long, legato sentences that do not confuse or exhaust the reader but instead impart delight, like a singer holding the note and drawing out the phrase? One man who made this question his life's work was an American professor of literature, Francis Christensen. His life story is soon told, so little of it is known. He was born in 1902, taught most of his career at the University of Southern California, and died in 1970. He was in his sixties, and near retirement, before he began publishing scholarly articles on writing. His reputation rests on one of them, "A Generative Rhetoric of the Sentence." It argues that this natural building block, the sentence, should be at the heart of teaching writing.

Given how little I can find out about him, I can't help wondering if Christensen was anything like the eponymous hero of John Williams's classic novel *Stoner*. There is at least one intriguing similarity: both of them went rogue. Bill Stoner teaches all his adult life in the English department at the University of Missouri. After a feud with his head of department he is assigned freshman composition, the unsexy option routinely farmed out to the untenured, who must teach bored students, doing other majors, about subclauses and adverbials. Stoner flings out the composition syllabus and starts teaching graduate-level stuff to a bunch of bewildered beginners.

In a different way, Christensen also flung out the composition syllabus—believing, as he said, that we were "making grammar too good for human nature's daily food." He felt that writing was mostly taught by telling students what they were doing wrong, and dividing the literate from the illiterate. Instead of helping everyone to communicate well, this method worked by excommunicating those who failed its strict initiation rites. The grammar books were just rules for "salvaging misbegotten sentences." Christensen's advice was to forget those books, for now. What did skilled writers, whom we read for pleasure and delight, do?

He traced his own sentence ideal back to the "Senecan amble." The Earl of Shaftesbury invented this term for the looser sentence shapes arising in the seventeenth century as English tried to free itself from a Latinate style. The Latinate ideal was the periodic sentence, the one Cicero used to keep an audience on edge, stacking clause on clause in pursuit of the main verb, which arrived like a punchline just before the full stop.

Milton imposed this Latin syntax even on his poetry. *Paradise Lost* turns the simple, additive style of Genesis into long sentences laden with clauses nesting inside each other like Russian dolls. The poem's first main verb, *sing*, appears only in line six, its first full stop ten lines later. Milton's prose sentences, buttressed with subordinating *whereins* and *whereofs*, often run to over a hundred words. When reading him you just have to dive in, hold your breath and, with each full stop, come up for air.

The Senecan amble, by contrast, took after Seneca's conversational, self-questing prose. It was a style suited to the early modern world—a fluid, curiosity-driven place in which many things once thought to be shaped by God or fate were now seen to be shaped by human whim. The Senecan amble tries to honor the liquid reality of this world and the ad hoc way we give it a shape in our heads. It begins the sentence by stating the main idea and then embroiders and particularizes it, sometimes changing its mind midway and starting anew. The French philosopher Blaise Pascal called this style "the painting of thought."

John Donne ambles, Seneca-like, in his sermons. His sentences are drawn-out conceits, long filaments of thought. They somehow bring together logic and gentleness, reason and passion, acerbity and receptivity. They move forward associatively, in allusive phrases that hold the attention briefly before the next phrase takes to the floor. They flaunt their learning but revel in the loose-fitting ligatures of speech and thought. Like his poetry, Donne's prose is a sort of heartfelt thinking. You can actually see him thinking and feeling on the page, working it out in front of you, as the writing moves and gathers force under the prickling itch of the moment.

Watch how this sentence, from a sermon Donne gave in 1627 about death, puzzles out its own purposes: "And into that gate they shall enter, and in that house they shall dwell, where there shall be no Cloud nor Sun, no darkness nor dazzling, but one equal light, no noise nor silence, but one equal music, no fears nor hopes, but one equal possession, no foes nor friends, but one equal communion and identity, no ends nor beginnings, but one equal eternity." Donne amplifies incrementally, adding synonyms and rephrasings, a technique then known as "heaping up," or he drags out a dizzy riff like a jazz musician. It is as if he is always scrabbling his way toward a beautiful truth just beyond reach.

•

According to Christensen, this seventeenth-century ideal of the sentence as a mind thinking along the page was slowly crushed in the eighteenth century—by a new style that sliced the world into logical sequence and served it up like a cold cut. The writing of high Augustan stylists like Edward Gibbon and Samuel Johnson suggests a ready-stocked and finely weighted mind, not a mind in motion. Even in his shorter sentences, Johnson will put a prepositional or noun phrase before the subject and main verb, so the point comes late. "Of the Epistle from Eloisa to Abelard, I do not know the date." "That it will immediately become popular I have not promised to myself." Of all the many kinds of maddening, these sentences can be the most.

Tidiness and order were foisted on the language. Alongside Johnson's *Dictionary* there were now hundreds of grammar books, catalogs of errors and gaucheries to avoid. One of these books, Lindley Murray's *English Grammar* of 1795, sold more than ten million copies. Their aim was to take writing as far as possible from the looseness and artlessness of speech. The ideal sentence was now multipart and premeditatedly elegant. The joyless school grammar tradition—the long conjugation of irregular verbs, or the parsing of sentences into their anatomical elements, chalked on squeaky blackboards in tedious afternoon double periods—starts here.

Since then, Christensen thought, a freer style had begun to prevail among professional writers, but not in the grammar books. The writing teachers were still stuck in the eighteenth century. They had forgotten that every sentence is really a song, the singing of a world into being. They thought of it now as a grammatical unit, and composition as the naming and assembling of parts. Christensen especially hated the schoolroom task of sentence combining. Here students had to make complex sentences out of two or more simple ones, piling on subordinations in an ill-starred search for complexity. It led to "pretzel prose": twisted knots of words, looping back on themselves and leaving the reader's mouth dry and full of salty crumbs.

•

The special scourge of modern writing, Christensen felt, was turning the subject of a sentence into a long noun phrase. This puts the reader on hold until he has unpicked it and got to the sentence's driver, the main verb. The more you read, the more you see that Christensen is right. The long noun phrase is the nemesis of clarity and ease in prose.

It comes from the perennial problem of trying to cram too much into the sentence, and especially into the subject. A long noun phrase can be infinitely long, embedding any number of other phrases within it. It soon becomes unclear what is modifying what: the road *next to the railway line* [adjectival phrase] *skirting the edge of the lake* [participial phrase] *that I drove on yesterday* [relative clause]. Worse, the long noun phrase just becomes a motionless word clump, which stops the sentence dead until you get to a verb. Sentences with long noun phrases as subjects can be perfectly correct and still virtually unreadable.

In a short sentence with a long noun phrase, the verb comes too late. *The time to stop wishing my life was perfect before it could truly begin had come.* That lopsided sentence has a very long subject, an auxiliary (*had*) and a main verb (*come*). Before you get your head round the thought, it has crashed into the full stop. But if you cut the noun phrase in two and stick the verb phrase in the middle, the sentence revives a little. *The time had come to stop wishing my life was perfect before it could truly begin.* The reader is no longer left hanging in midair, waiting for the verb.

With longer sentences the problem is harder to fix. Academic writing likes to build up long noun phrases by linking words with prepositions, like "the *x* that needs *to* be read *as* located *in* an ambivalence *around*" or "the reconfiguration *of x to* preclude the possibility *of x*." When prepositions come too close together like this, the sentence turns into an arrhythmic rattlebag of words. It just inches sideways, crab-like, until it stops.

Student writers often come unstuck with prepositions. They write things like *This essay is going to explore into how* or *What this means is upon the reader to decide*. Prepositions are small and harmless-looking words that cause untold confusion because they have so many roles. They relate words to each other by space, time, direction, cause, purpose or association. And they refer to actual relationships (*in* London, *at* the cinema) or idiomatic ones (*in* a daze, *at* a loss). In limp writing, they can shift invisibly from explaining literal relationships to metaphorical ones and be used to hint at connections without having to think them through. They can also multitask confusingly as other parts of speech. Be wary of *as* as a preposition, as it can also be an adverb and a conjunction.

Strings of prepositions make for dull sounds and ponderous rhythms—and they are hard for a writer to weed out because they are so small that they become invisible, like the dangerously versatile *of*. Academic writing loves *of* phrases such as *in terms of*, *the role of* or *the process of*. Too many *ofs* in a long sentence means that they are staple-gunning nouns together with too few verbs. A word-processing algorithm that spotted preposition overkill, especially one that rooted out all those *ofs*, would be better than a spellcheck. Prepositions are a bad way to stitch up long sentences because they neither connect phrases clearly, like conjunctions, nor separate them clearly, like punctuation. They are the worst of both worlds.

•

The secret with long sentences, Christensen said, was to set their heart beating at once by putting the subject and main verb at the start. If the reader can't identify the sentence's subject and main verb—or worse, which is not uncommon, the writer can't—it will never begin to make sense. A sentence gets its thrust by moving from subject to action; interrupting this through-line takes some of the thrust away. The reader expects the subject to be followed by the verb, and is confused if you put too many words between them. If you separate the subject and verb, that intervening matter will be read as an interruption, with the reader left dangling until resolution arrives. If the intervening matter is long, you are probably using it to say something important. But the reader will still read it distractedly, scurrying toward the verb.

If you swiftly deliver the main news of the sentence, the subject and verb, then the rest of the sentence can unfurl itself less hurriedly. Christensen called this the "cumulative sentence." In class, he gave his students a simple subject and main verb and got them to attach "free modifiers" to it. He called them this to distinguish them from bound modifiers, like adverbs and adjectives, which fit in specific slots in the sentence. Free modifiers are loose additive phrases that fit more freely around the main clause. They can be put almost anywhere in the sentence and shrunk and stretched to adjust its rhythm.

Modern writing relies a lot on these free modifiers. Sentences a few hundred years ago were not only much longer, they used more full clauses and more words like *whereby, whereof* and *therewith* to link them up. These words are now rare and even simple relative pronouns like *that* and *which* appear less often. Writing uses lighter syntactical cement, without all the *wherefores* and *upon whiches*. A sentence gets convoluted when it has lots of relative clauses—beginning with *who, which* and *that*—making up longer noun phrases. Replace these with free modifiers and it not only saves words, it also makes the links looser and easier to untie. Free modifying is a sort of invisible subordination, dispensing with the need for full clauses.

Christensen analyzed the writing in *Harper's* magazine— writing that people had paid to read, so it had an incentive to be clear. More than half the sentences were cumulative. A quarter of these began with a brief adverbial or prepositional phrase. The rest began with the subject and main verb and then moved down into the detail. Given how skilled writers write, Christensen concluded, those teachers who urged their students to vary their sentence openings should stop doing it. They should tell them, instead, to start with the subject and verb to establish what the sentence is about, and then, with free modifiers, take that thing that it is about over to the window and turn it around in the light.

Write a plain sentence. *Spiders are loners.* Then just add a phrase, and keep adding. *Spiders are loners, working at night to build their webs, cross-hatched creations best seen on dewy mornings, each silken strand shining with water beads, the whole edifice flimsy enough to be destroyed by a stray human leg, and yet, in its filigree and symmetry, a thing of beauty, and also of utility, for this lone spider will spend its whole life in contact with its self-made silk—tightening its lines, slinging lassoes and awaiting its prey.*

A cumulative sentence starts with the simple thing and then unwraps the more intricate things in little, manageable layers. It spreads the reader's brain load over the length of the sentence, asking her to understand it as she goes along. Once the basics are down, it takes flight, and tracks the mind's motion as it snatches at meaning on the fly.

Try again. *The giraffe nibbled the acacia leaves.* Add to it. *The giraffe nibbled the acacia leaves, stretching its neck to browse for the thornless ones at the top of the tree, all the while surveying the veldt, batting its long eyelashes at no one in particular, giving not a thought to how its short-necked ancestors strove in vain to reach these lofty branches before natural selection did its happy work, if indeed that is why giraffes have long necks, for in fact they do much of their munching near the ground, and some giraffe experts believe that their necks evolved as weapons, so that they could swing their heads at each other*

*like maces and kill with one blow, a giraffe's skull weighing as much as
a bag of cement.*

The cumulative sentence is the prose equivalent of the long
tracking shot, that signature piece of technical virtuosity loved by
film directors. Joe Wright's film *Atonement* has one beautiful, five-
and-a-half-minute, one-shot glide across the beach at Dunkirk.
The camera follows three soldiers, led by James McAvoy, picking
their way through the smoke, rubble and confusion—with soldiers
brawling, sunbathing, shooting horses, destroying cars, burning
papers and singing hymns, while a Ferris wheel turns in the distance. All the way through, McAvoy's sunken eyes and stunned
expression guide you through the chaos and tell you where to
look. The whole shot is like a long, zigzag sentence that never loses
sight of its end. The viewer gets a sense, just as the reader gets in an
elegantly long sentence, of both plenitude and simultaneity, of different strands of life unfolding thrillingly in unison.

•

Free modifiers can be lots of different things: participial phrases,
prepositional phrases, clusters of adjectives. But the simplest and
easiest free modifier to master is the appositive. Appositives are
nouns or noun phrases that rename the noun or noun phrase
alongside them. The park bench provides solace, *a moment of
stillness in the stir of city life.* Unlike a premodifying adjective, the
appositive comes after the noun and propels the sentence
forward—just as we do in speech, clarifying as we go along. Do
you remember that guy, *the one we saw in the cafe with the man bun
and the neck tattoos?* On the surface the appositive is just renam-
ing the noun, but underneath it is refining, adding texture and
telling a little story, like an elongated adjective. Rock pools are
tutorials in biodiversity, *the gift that life has for enduring and thriv-
ing in uncongenial places.*

Sometimes the shift between a main and a relative clause is
too abrupt. *I finally faced my dread of the e-mail inbox that had lived*

with me since the weekend. An appositive smooths it out, providing a little bridge from the clause to the phrase, so *that* is not doing all the heavy lifting. *I finally faced my dread of the e-mail inbox, a tight knot of fear that had lived with me since the weekend.* You can make a similar bridge just by revisiting a noun. *I finally faced my dread of the e-mail inbox, a dread that had lived with me since the weekend.* The repeated noun is some other word than the subject, such as the object, hidden in a weaker part of the clause. The sentence stops at the cliff-edge of the comma, mulls over which bit of the main clause needs more attention, then, in the phrase that follows, rescues and enlarges on it.

A trickier modifier to master, but even more flexible, is the absolute—from the Latin *absolūtus*, meaning "free and unconstrained." The absolute combines a noun phrase with a participial phrase and stands syntactically apart from the rest of the sentence, linked only by that thinnest of threads, a comma. *I gaze at the dead leaves, their yellow-brown mulch littering the gutters.* Absolutes are useful for doing away with weak linking verbs and conjunctions. *My work for the day was done and I raided the fridge. My work for the day done, I raided the fridge.*

The absolute is almost a full sentence, because it has its own subject (the noun phrase). All that stops it from being a sentence is its use of a participle rather than a finite verb. Being so nearly independent of the main clause, it gives the writer great freedom. Unlike the appositive, it does not just modify the noun next to it; it modifies the whole clause, so can be stuck almost anywhere. *His stomach churning,* the professor faced the crowd of angry students. The professor, *his stomach churning,* faced the crowd of angry students. The professor faced the crowd of angry students, *his stomach churning.*

•

These loose chains of phrases have to be well punctuated, so the reader can separate them clearly in his head. In the cumulative sentence, the comma is king—and the comma is the hardest punctuation mark to get right. You cannot just rely on grammar when dispensing commas, but must have osmotically absorbed their effects in other people's writing, for the tiny pause they hold within them is so much a matter of ear. *The forks went missing, then the spoons.* The most delicate commas are very nearly comma splices. *Our comforts are many, our joys few.* A single comma in a sentence can carry much of its meaning. *I went to the lawnmower museum, alone.*

A comma is the least invasive mark and the most pliable. Commas separate phrases when the syntax alone is not enough to make their relationship clear. A comma lights up the edifice of a sentence by corralling some of its words together and dividing them from others. Commas are hard to get right in long sentences because they have taken on the burden, once assumed by ungainly conjunctions and relative clauses, of unscrambling our thoughts. The longer the sentence, the more crucial the commas.

In a cumulative sentence, the commas come in parenthetical pairs to set apart the loose, modifying phrases. Student writers often do not know how to add these loose phrases to a main clause. So they end up linking clauses together with comma splices. *The problem with the comma splice is simple, it is not emphatic enough to join two independent clauses like this.* The comma splice sounds wrong because it marks off part of the sentence (*The problem with the comma splice is simple*) that should end with a stress. A comma can't create stress, because it has so many possible roles that we have to read beyond it to work out what it is doing there. A comma says, simply, "read on." It hurries us forward into what follows.

A comma-splice sentence can be fixed by replacing the comma with a semicolon, a colon, a conjunction or a full stop. But often the problem runs deeper: habitual comma-splicers can't tell the difference between a clause and a phrase. A clause needs a subject and a main verb, and can form a sentence as long as it is not subordinate to another clause. A phrase cannot form a sentence on its own but can, if linked to a main clause, extend one. Often all that is needed to divide a phrase from a clause, or another phrase, is a comma. And since a comma requires the reader to read on to make sense of it, it is perfect for driving the sentence forward into the next phrase.

A comma is not the only way of dividing up a long sentence. Parentheses and dashes let you pull out a phrase so it can be read apart from the main thought, making the whole sentence easier to unload. Parenthesizing a phrase off puts less stress on it than placing it between commas; dashes put more stress on it. Imagine reading the sentence aloud. You drop your voice to bridge over words in parentheses (*to signal that this is a slightly sotto voce sideshow to the main thought*) and then resume a normal tone. But you raise your voice when bridging over words in dashes—*like this bit that I want to stress because I am getting into my stride now*—to play up what they enclose.

Either way, such parenthetical and dash-marked asides are their own little self-governing realms. Parentheses and dashes interrupt a sentence without otherwise affecting it. As a brief holiday from linearity, they can sluice a long sentence that might feel congested with just commas in it. They also give writing a voice, because this is what we do in talk, butting in on our own train of thought before picking it up again. The sentence seems to be talking to us more intimately, muttering under its breath or musing into the air.

Overused, though, parentheses and dashes can make writing feel as if it is permanently interrupting itself. Commas are still the most useful mark in a long sentence because, unlike parentheses and dashes, they make no difference to the stress. They just carry the reader along, gifting her the tiny pause she needs to break the sentence up into digestible pieces. Only when you learn to separate clauses and phrases properly with commas can you write long sentences of lucidity and grace.

•

A long sentence should feel like it is pushing at its edges while still keeping its shape. All along its length it will feel ever so slightly chaotic but still composed, never losing its underlying order. It helps if it does not seem too eager to resolve itself, and yet manages to inspire confidence that, eventually, whatever its wild detours and exotic interludes, it will.

The longer it gets, though, the harder it will be to land it well. A cumulative sentence, because it has used up the main verb early on, can easily peter out into a long, waggy tail of free modifiers. Aristotle, who preferred the periodic sentence, thought a loose one "unpleasant because it is endless, for all wish to have the end in sight."

One solution is to put the longest phrase last, after the reader's work of unpicking the rest of the sentence is done. At the start of a sentence, where it forms the subject and delays the main verb, the long noun phrase is the reader's enemy. But at the end of a sentence, when most of the untangling of sense is done, it is the reader's friend. Swallowed in one gulp, it quickens the pace as the full stop heaves into view. A heavy noun phrase at the end makes a sentence feel over with and irrevocable. The funereal cry of the herring gull has long fed *the anthropomorphic myth that these birds house the souls of sailors drowned at sea.*

Think of the sentence climbing slowly up its syntactical hill before rolling down quickly to the full stop at the bottom. The seventeenth-century writer Thomas Browne traded in these up-and-down-the-hill sentences, sometimes resting at the top to admire the view: "Time, which antiquates antiquities [up the hill], and hath an art to make dust of all things [at the top], hath yet spared these minor monuments [down again]." As it rolls down, the reader knows the hard work is done. He no longer has to do the equivalent of contracting his calves, lifting his body weight against gravity to reach the top. The sentence just falls away, but quickly, and hence strongly. A more suspenseful way to roll down the hill is with a single dash and a short, solving phrase. The dash heralds a downshift in the thought without the need for a wordy link, and signals that the sentence is near its end—*for which your reader will give thanks.*

Ending your sentence with a list of three also lands it well. For neurologically vague reasons, the human mind is fond of framing reality thus. Perhaps it is because three is the smallest number with a rhythm. Rhythm is not just the beat but the spaces between the beat—so you need at least two spaces, and hence three beats, to create it. With three things, you can set up a pattern, then break it. Tension is created, built and resolved. A quest story has three narrative phases: departure, adventure, return. Jokes have a set-up, reiteration and punchline. A twelve-bar-blues singer sings a first line, repeats it and then improvises a third, longer line. The blues, like most popular music, is built around three chords. "Country music," the songwriter Harlan Howard said, "is three chords and the truth." Fairy tales follow the same rule of three. The princess guesses Rumpelstiltskin's name on the third go. The three little pigs build houses of straw, wood and brick. The three bears have three chairs, three beds and three bowls of porridge.

In his essay "The Rhetoric of the Series," Winston Weathers suggests that a tripartite list falls sweetly between the two poles of excessive certainty and chaotic abundance. A list of two things suggests that nothing more need be said. A list of four or more suggests something diffuse and uncontainable. But a list of three sounds like a plausible sample without being unruly. And if you expand the number of syllables with each item, the strongest stress falls on the third and longest thing. The first two are little running jumps and, as you unclench the rhythmic grip by adding to the unstressed syllables, it feels as if the sentence is just slightly running away from itself. All I could find in the fridge was *half a cucumber, some festering Camembert and an unopened bag of wilted arugula leaves.*

These techniques for ending long sentences all have the same aim. They give the reader a heads-up that the sentence is coming to a close, and has just this one last thing to say. In their essay "The Science of Scientific Writing," George Gopen and Judith Swan argue that, as we start to read each new sentence, we take a "mental breath." When we come to a comma or semicolon in the middle of the sentence—a little waystation on the path to overall sense—we exhale that mental breath slightly and take another, mini breath. But we don't begin to fully exhale that mental breath until we sense that the sentence is coming to a close.

In a short sentence this moment of syntactic closure can start just a word or short phrase from the end; in a long sentence it can start with a list that goes on for several lines. Whichever, the moment begins when the reader knows that the only thing left in the sentence is this last piece of the puzzle. We read words faster than we say them, so our mental breath has more capacity than our actual breath. And yet, just as with lung power, there are limits. However pleasing a sentence is to read, its full stop, which declares that all the parsing is done and that we can now draw breath, always comes as a relief. The longer the sentence, the greater the relief. The reader has been liberated, briefly, from the work of reading.

•

Every writer is a poet by default and every sentence a little poem. The longer the sentence, the more closely it resembles poetry, or should. A good training exercise for the long-sentence writer is to read some of the countless poems written as one long sentence, often just a simple collection of modifiers. Henry Vaughan's "The Night" has no main verbs or connectives, just a lightly tied bale of appositives that rename the noun in the poem's title: "this world's defeat; The stop to busy fools." George Herbert's "Prayer" repeats the trick: "the soul in paraphrase, heart in pilgrimage."

American poetry, from Walt Whitman to Amy Clampitt, offers a vast lending library of these one-sentence poems that pile up free modifiers parted by commas. When you start to read poems for their sentences, you see how many are cumulative—how they run over many lines, or the whole poem, inviting us to wonder at how much they can fit inside themselves, and whether they will ever be an adequate vessel for all that needs to be said.

In fact, a cumulative sentence turns into a poem if you just add line breaks:

> The London Underground
> marks the hardest of borders
> between tourist and native:
> the tourist fumbling for change,
> squinting at the ticket machine
> and trying to work out
> which zone he is in,
> then flinching at the barrier
> as if unsure it will open for him,
> while the native absently
> places her card on the reader,
> and walks straight through
> in one balletic action,
> knowing the exact moment it will open
> without even breaking her stride,
> and then gauging the spot on the platform
> at which the doors will open,
> and answering the beeping sound
> that announces the closing of the doors
> by instinctively contorting her body
> to fit inside the carriage,
> pulled along by habit
> and the momentum
> of other moving bodies,
> as at home in her habitat
> as a swift on the wing.

Poems, like songs sung well, are made of sentences as well as lines. The sentence is part of a poem's music just as much as the meter. Line and meter are the flimsy frame behind which the unassailable syntactical rhythms of the English sentence rumble on. For many poets, the unit of composition is not the line but the sentence spoken in a single outbreath. Robert Graves said that a poem came to him in "the usual line-and-a-half that unexpectedly forces itself on the entranced mind." Poets write in sentences, just like everyone else, then play them off against the meter. Meter, like rhyme, is so strict that it has to pull against something to create its agreeable tensions. Without sentences, poetry would just be singsong.

Think of a long sentence as a poem and it will always be clear because each part of it will unravel in little musical phrases, with all the different parts coloring one another without it ever feeling discordant. The one indispensable quality in a long sentence is that it divide into these little pieces. It does not have to be loose and cumulative; in fact, it can have lots of subordination and the verb can be left to the end like a Ciceronian period. But it must cut up into these smaller pieces to be chewed and swallowed one at a time, and still always be moving, with each short phrase, toward completion. A long sentence should feel alive, awake, kinetic, aerobic—like a poem.

•

For Francis Christensen, learning to write was also learning to live. He believed that teaching his students how to write a really great long sentence could teach them to "look at life with more alertness." It should not just be about ensuring that the sentence is grammatically correct, or even clear. The one true aim was "to enhance life—to give the self (the soul) body by wedding it to the world, to give the world life by wedding it to the self." He wanted his students to become "sentence acrobats" who could "dazzle by their syntactic dexterity."

Another fan of the Senecan amble, the poet Elizabeth Bishop, liked sentences that "attempted to dramatize the mind in action rather than in repose." In an essay she wrote for *Vassar Review* in 1934 while still a student, Bishop explored how Gerard Manley Hopkins catches and preserves "the movement of an idea—the point being to crystallize it early enough so that it still has movement." A single stanza of Hopkins could be, she wrote, "as full of, aflame with, motion as one of Van Gogh's cedar trees."

Bishop's own poems are like that. Spoken by a restlessly darting, apprehensive voice, they live inside their cumulative sentences, loose trails of words full of qualifications, self-corrections and second thoughts. Bishop, too, thought of the long-sentence writer as an aerial artist. Her favorite lines from Hopkins were "reminiscent of the caprice of a perfectly trained acrobat: falling through the air to snatch his partner's ankles he can yet, within the fall, afford an extra turn and flourish in safety, without spoiling the form of his flight."

I like this metaphor but am not quite persuaded by it. Is the writer of a long sentence really like an acrobat? Should a long sentence be as showboating as the turns and tumbles of the trapeze artist? I side more with Thoreau, who warned the writer against "trying to turn too many feeble somersaults in the air." And I am reminded of Burt Lancaster and Tony Curtis in *Trapeze*, attempting to draw reverential gasps from the increasingly bored circus crowds, while down below an elephant stands on its hind legs or a bear rides a bicycle. A trapeze act is all jumpy, interrupted suspense—the somersault over as quickly as it is seen, with that awkward smack as the anchorman grabs the forearms of his flying partner and the ropes quiver. I am not sure I want to write sentences like that, more death-cheating jeopardy than unforced elegance. And if learning to write is also learning to live, then I don't want to live like that either.

•

A better metaphor for the long-sentence writer, perhaps, is the high-wire walker. I know that will sound overblown, perhaps deluded. A writer is not risking all, as did the young Frenchman Philippe Petit one August day in 1974, when he secretly strung a wire cable between the twin towers of the World Trade Center and walked across it in the morning rush hour, a quarter of a mile above a street in Lower Manhattan. And yet Petit made the comparison himself. On the steps of the courthouse after his arrest for this illegal act, he shouted, "I am not a daredevil, I am a writer in the sky!"

The trick, with both a long sentence and a high-wire walk, is to give off an air of controlled anarchy, of boundless freedom within clear constraints. Wire-walking may be a little more perilous than writing, but both are, ultimately, all about technique. Petit prepared like a scholar for his New York walk, studying photographs, calculating the effects of high winds and building sway, sneaking into the building to case the joint and recce the anchor points. But once he stepped out on to that thin steel cable he had to rely, like the sentence writer, on learned instinct, got through assiduous rehearsal. The high-wire artist must arrange his body so that it fights the wire's urge to rotate, like any cylinder, when stepped on. He must teach his feet to land on the cable in such a way as to absorb its swaying and then coax his center of mass to move up to his torso, using his ankles as the pivot point. He must remember to pass the wire between his big and second toe, along the sole and behind the middle of the heel.

A high-wire walk has the rhythm and momentum of a long sentence. "I don't see fear in my life," Petit said. "That's how people die: they are frozen rather than acting and thinking." The walk, like a sentence, takes place in time as well as space. It cannot be done all at once, and succeeds only if it is in constant motion. The high-wire walker must be ever alert and dynamic— although, like a sentence writer putting in a comma or semicolon, he can pause at the cavaletti, the anchor ropes that create little oases of three-dimensional steadiness and stop the wire swaying too much.

In the middle of the wire between the twin towers, as if neatly punctuating a sentence, Petit knelt, lay on his back and waved at the puzzled birds hovering over him. The crowds of people gazing up from the streets below relaxed a little, but could not quite exhale. As Petit neared the South Tower they began to breathe out, and as he made it there they sighed with relief—at least until he turned round and did the whole thing again, making seven more crossings before surrendering to the waiting police. Eight sentences: a high-wire paragraph.

As a metaphor, *walking a tightrope* means treading a fine line, living on the edge. But Petit was not interested in this death-defying aspect of high-wire walking. He refused to wear a safety harness, not because it would make the walk safer, but because it would be "inelegant." He also refused to play to the crowd as a big-top tightrope walker might, by making it all look harder than it was, or pretending to lose his balance and nearly fall. Not for him the stunts of Blondin at Niagara Falls, walking the wire on stilts, blindfold or pushing a wheelbarrow. It was as if he were doing it all for his own amusement and for anyone who just happened to be looking on. Even after the walk he employed no agent, refusing to trade it for money or renown. It was simply, as Paul Auster put it, "a gift of astonishing, indelible beauty to New York."

•

A long sentence too should be a beautiful, indelible gift. It should give pleasure without provisos, not buttonhole and bedazzle the reader with virtuosity. It can put the reader on edge a little, so long as this does not feel like its main point, so long as it feels as if the sentence has no ulterior motive other than the giving of its own life-delighting self. This is what readability scores will never tell you. They deal only with reading ease, not the knottier, exacting pleasures of expectancy and surprise, the teasing way that long sentences suspend the moment of closure.

I am a fully terrestrial being, afraid of flying and scared of heights. On the top floors of tall buildings, I don't even like being close to the windows. I could no more walk on a tightrope between two towers than I could flap my arms and fly across. Just looking at photos of Petit on that wire makes my legs wobble. But how I would love some day to be able to write a sentence of such pointless, big-hearted, joy-bestowing beauty, one that would make a stranger drop what they were doing and, in the middle of a crowded street, look up.

6.

Foolish Like a Trout

Or how to join sentences together with invisible thread

In 1979 one of the early word-processing programs, WordStar, launched, with an exciting new feature. The control key, the only non-typewriter key that most computer keyboards had back then, could be used to cut and paste. *Cut and paste* was named after a procedure done traditionally with scissors and glue. Writers would slice up their draft paragraphs, rearrange them into a new order with a glue stick, retype it all into the next draft and start over again. Stationers sold editing scissors, with blades long enough to cut the width of a sheet of paper with one snip. The word-processor pictograph for *cut* is still a pair of scissors. It looks as quaint now as the envelope icon on e-mails.

WordStar's cut-and-paste commands let this hitherto messy operation happen with a few clicks. John McPhee called his first computer, bought in 1984, "a five-thousand-dollar pair of scissors." Now we could write in the nonlinear way we think, laying down insights as they burst and worrying about their order later. But like every improving invention, cut and paste had its decriers accusing it of making things worse. They feared that it disturbed the natural flow of writing, the groove we get into when one sentence just seems to call up the next. They worried that the ease of reordering words, and the invitation to overcorrect, would scramble our inborn feel for sequential prose.

There is no evidence that this happened. If it had, then, as part of the last generation for whom writing was inescapably analog, I should be a witness for the prosecution. I was born a year before Intel released the microprocessor that started the personal computer revolution, but two decades before word processors arrived on every work desk. At school we still had those old wooden desks with a hole in one corner for the inkwell. Not that we needed it, ours being the age of pencils with chewed eraser tips and cheap plastic ballpoints with see-through, leaky ink reservoirs. But writing remained a slow, tactile, untidy affair. At the end of each school day our fingers were calloused and our palms covered with inky smudges.

We even had handwriting lessons, getting ticks for neatness and crosses for clumsiness in our double-lined exercise books. In these classes the guiding hand of the great handwriting expert, Marion Richardson, could still be felt. A former art teacher, Richardson thought that children's innate delight in drawing and scribbling was the best way for them to acquire a smooth, legible hand. In her 1935 book *Writing and Writing Patterns*, she claimed that the urge to draw and to write grows out of the same thing: the hand gestures we use naturally in unrehearsed speech. In human evolution, these gestures came before talking. You can always tell if someone on TV is using a teleprompter, because they never move their hands.

Those writers who still cling to the pen over the keyboard are Richardson's heirs. They feel intuitively that their thoughts run best from their brain to their looping hand, that writing flows most easily from one word to the next in the motions of cursive script. Most of the generation below me, which includes the students I teach, would not know how to frame such a thought, never mind think it. For them, writing longhand is going the way of illuminated script or calligraphy. After three hours in an exam hall, they nurse their aching arms. The touchscreen has hyper-evolved their texting thumbs and atrophied their writing wrists.

No doubt these young people, like those recalcitrant handwriters, will feel sentimental about the glass squares they now stare at habitually when some other technology supplants them, as it will. For writers of every generation grow attached to which-ever physical implements they use to make their sentences—just as musicians grow to love their instruments.

•

In his book *Piano Notes* the writer and musician Charles Rosen writes of his physical need to play the piano. He likens it to the thrill a tennis player gets from hitting the ball, from feeling that thwack of rubber, nylon and pressurized air against the racket's tensioned strings. It is not enough, he writes, for pianists just to love the sound of the notes. They must have "a genuine love for the mechanics and difficulties of playing, a physical need for the contact with the keyboard."

A certain kind of composer looks down on writing at a piano. Berlioz was proud of not being able to play one; Schubert could write music on the back of restaurant menus. These purists think that composers should be able to compose in their heads, without the crutch of a keyboard. But to Rosen, they are stuck in the Cartesian dualism that sees the body as inferior to the mind and denies our animal selves. No singer would ever make such a mistake. They know that a voice is not merely a neutral carrier of the words and tune. It is an instrument to be handled with as much care as a cello. In an interview Rosen put it more bluntly: "Pianists are like tenors—we're very stupid; they like to feel their voices, we like to feel the ivory under our fingers."

Whether or not they are as stupid as pianists and tenors, writ-ers are the same. They like working with their tools, hearing their own voices, feeling the ivory under their fingers. Just as singers do vocal workouts, and pianists five-finger exercises, so writers seem to need the calisthenic routines of writing. Even working in that translucent medium, a screen, they like to feel they are chiseling words into shape. The first computer I wrote with was a snail-slow, ugly-beige-box Amstrad with eye-straining green letters on a black screen. But I can still recall, more than thirty years later, what a thrill it was to amend a sentence and see the paragraph reshape itself like flowing water. Or to discover that the last word of each line "wrapped"—jumped down automatically to the start of the next one—with no need to press return, a little conjuring trick that felt worthy of a cymbal crash.

The Barbadian writer Kamau Brathwaite was just as electrified when he got his first computer, an Apple Macintosh. He saw straight away that it could be a way of returning to the fluid orality of the Caribbean literary tradition, so long suppressed by the formal fixity of the printed word. He called word processing "writing in light." In those heady early days, many of us saw it like that. We loved the screen's luminosity, its phosphors bright enough to burn ghost letters into the glass, and the hard drive's near silence, its low, refrigerator hum. This was writing not with noise, the Kalashnikov clatter of the typewriter keys and the interposing ping of the carriage return, but with light. The digital historian Matthew Kirschenbaum notes that, had the camera not got there first, we might have named word processing after the Greek for "light writing": *photography*.

This early enchantment with the digital has long since faded, to be replaced by nostalgia for the analog. Some blame the decline of handwriting for a decline in the ability to construct flowing sentences. Others grieve for similar reasons over the loss of the typewriter, which was even more linear a writing tool than the pen. Short of cutting it up and pasting it back together, the only way to correct a typewritten draft was to drown it in Wite-Out or to start again. This, they believe (surely in hindsight), concentrated the mind.

Hence the recent, niche trend for what Kirschenbaum calls "austerity-ware": minimalist word-processing programs that deliver a full-screen, decluttered writing surface like the word processors of yore. These programs offer no cut and paste, not even a backspace. All you can do is save, print and type, in retro-chic green-on-black letters in Courier font. You cannot help but write in straight lines, starting in the screen's top left-hand corner and working your way to the bottom right.

Even if I believed, which I don't, that the computer upset one's natural flow, whatever that is, austerity-ware would still feel to me like trying to stuff the toothpaste back in the tube. It seeks a magical solution to something that always was and always will be hard. Getting writing to flow is so laborious that we put our faith in charms and talismans that might make it easier. Some swear by a pencil with a particular hardness of graphite, others by the latest laptop with backlit keyboard and shiny chrome. We are all searching for the one utensil that will give our writing the elusive flow of inspiration, while making it easy to reshuffle and start all over again. In other words, and as usual, we want the best of both worlds.

•

All of which is a roundabout way of saying that so far this book has been based on a lie. The lie is that sentences work on their own, without need of other sentences. The truth is that the sentence you are reading needs the already read and the still unread sentences around it. A sentence is a social animal; it feeds off its fellows to form higher units of sense. A sentence needs a full stop not just to be a sentence, but so the next one can begin. Behind the search for "flow" in writing lies this feeling that sentences do not really count until they come together and turn aphoristic isolation into forward motion.

Because sentences have to live alongside each other, not every one can be as acoustically thrilling as the next. If this happens the reader gets weary. As Macaulay said of reading Seneca, it is like dining on nothing but anchovy sauce—or, as Clive James wrote of writing made only of killer sentences, like being constantly flicked with a wet towel. A dazzling sentence with no need of its neighbors is stealing too much of the light and may be so incandescent that it stops the reader in her tracks. Each sentence should burn brightly but briefly, lighting the way into the next one.

Between every sentence there is a tiny gap, marked by a full stop and a space, over which logic must leap. If the gap is too wide, the sentences are cast adrift from each other and the reader flails around in a sea of unrelated thought. If the gap is too narrow, and the link between the sentences too cumbrous, the reader is being spoonfed a connection she could have made herself. Inept writers leave gaps that are too wide, so the sentences seem irretrievably stranded from each other. But many competent writers leave gaps that are too narrow. Sentences need some space and silence between them, so the reader can see the full stop and hear its click.

Since all writing is really creative writing, we can learn much from writers of fiction about how to knit sentences together, whether we write fiction or not. The American writer and writing teacher John Gardner calls it "profluence": a smooth flow. A stubborn truth about all writing, for Gardner, is that it takes time to read. No one can read a story in an instant, so they need to feel it moving forward as they read it in time. Gardner doesn't just mean the plot, the causal chain of events in a story that pulls you along. He means the verbal music, the way the sentences click and clack together. A piece of writing does not need a what-happens-next to hook its reader; it just needs to feel as if its sentences are flowing ever on.

A single sentence takes time to read, and must gradually solve itself in the space it takes up on the page. So must a group of sentences. Writing refuses us the synchronicities of other art forms: the chords and harmonies of a song, the choreographed unity of a group of dancers, the broad canvas of a painting, the *mise-en-scène* of a film, or a spectacular building taken in with a sharp inward breath. Writing cannot reveal itself all at once but must write a world slowly into life. So it should feel like it is always going somewhere, but steadily, at the pace of reading, amassing detail and mood in a way that adds to what has gone before. The journey happens a word, a phrase, a sentence at a time.

•

The editor and writing teacher Gordon Lish had a theory about how sentences should fit together. He called it "consecution" Lish thought that storytelling worked best when the writer kept returning to and revising the previous sentence, in escalating, tautening patterns of sameness and variation. Consecution moves forward by looking backward, wheedling life and interest out of what was left unsaid in previous sentences. Letters and sounds from one sentence carry into the next, making the words come together at some barely noticed micro-level. Every word, every sentence, comes out of the last one—whether building on it, restating it, overturning it or shoving it unceremoniously aside. A sentence needs to say something compelling on its own, but leave enough unsaid in it to suggest the next one.

One of Lish's students, the short-story writer Gary Lutz, was inspired by this idea. In 2008 he gave a lecture to the writing program at Columbia University titled "The Sentence is a Lonely Place." Lutz explained to the students that as a reader he longed to read, and as a writer longed to write, stories in which "the sentence is a complete, portable solitude, a minute immediacy of consummated language." He wanted to read books that he could open at any page and find a sentence—"a totality, an omnitude, unto itself"—that gave him something beautiful and illuminating and cherishable all on its own.

Lutz's stories, if you try to summarize them, sound like nothing much. Their narrators and protagonists are lonely, nameless people in collapsing states of coupledom, permanently discomfited with their bodies and the various fluids they emit from their various apertures. But in these stories the usual elements—theme, setting, storyline—are just offshoots of the sentences.

The characters set foot out of the sound and shape of the words rubbing against each other. The sentence may be a lonely place, but a group of sentences can make fresh meanings out of the convergence of their collective solitude.

Amy Hempel, another student of Lish's, writes short stories that seem like plotless vignettes, just like Lutz's, but that hold the reader throughout. Her trick is to write a killer first line, the line that Lish calls "the attack." In "Nashville Gone to Ashes": "After the dog's cremation, I lie in my husband's bed and watch the Academy Awards for animals." In "Breathing Jesus": "Things turned around after I saw the breathing Jesus." In "Du Jour": "The first three days are the worst, they say, but it's been two weeks, and I'm still waiting for those first three days to be over." Hempel's first sentences are like Lutz's lonely places: they almost read as short stories in their own right, but they also demand a second sentence, which will in turn demand a third, and so on. Lish called this "torquing." The story is like a mainspring, and each sentence gives a little turn on the ratchet, steadily ramping up the stakes.

A lot of contemporary writing (not just fiction) is like this: the sentences seem hardly linked to each other at all but some invisible thread connects them. If your single sentences have enough life and interest in them—with "every step an arrival," as Rilke put it—they will hold the reader and then suggest ways that they can proceed. And if you move forward associatively in a way that *acts* as if it were sequential, you may find a hidden unity that has no need of the mucilage of linking phrases.

The aim is to make each sentence count, to cut down on the ones that are just treading water or only there to get from one bit to the next. Those are the sentences readers skim. If you treat the sentence as a lonely place it makes it easier, oddly, to move on to the next one. You achieve flow by fretting about it less. Each sentence is like a tidal island that looks cut off until, at low tide, a causeway to the mainland appears.

Make each sentence worth reading and something in it will lead you into the next one. You will find that you can get away with turn-on-a-dime movements and unscheduled flights into new terrain without much linking apparatus. The reader's interest in each succeeding sentence will whip up the energy to carry them through. Write the sentence that emerges or transpires out of the last one, instead of linking back to it via some scaffold of logic you have built separately from the sentences themselves.

•

While writing this chapter I have been playing, on a loop, the jazz pianist Bill Evans's beautiful seven-minute tone poem, "Peace Piece." I never tire of trying to work it out. It starts with a slow-rocking, two-chord, left-hand ostinato—a persistent phrase that runs throughout. As these soft chords undulate, a decorative line unfolds on Evans's right hand, growing lusher as it changes key and turns unexpected corners, moving up and down the right half of the keyboard, all glissandos and answering chimes, becoming quicker as the left hand stays slow. Evans has a lovely legato line, never releasing a note until it has fully played out, so the tones overlap lushly in the soundboard. At the end of the piece he unites the right and left hand at last and the ostinato turns into a resolving chord.

Amazingly, the whole thing was improvised in one take (although there is some debate about how much it may have been practiced beforehand). The ostinato began as a simple back-and-forth vamp to introduce Leonard Bernstein's song "Some Other Time," but Evans got stuck on it and it grew into something else. "It started to get so much of its own feeling and identity," he said, "that I just figured, well, I'll keep going."

Just keep going. This, it seems to me, is the musical form of what Lish calls "consecution." Each note, each chord, each phrase arises out of the last. Evans has a knack for making something fresh out of stock chord sequences, warping or slanting them slightly into startling shapes, mixing the triadic with the atonal. Like many great works of art, "Peace Piece" does not shout for attention; it just joins the flow of life and draws you in. It seems to drift into the air and yet stay grounded, gently circling round the same idea and yet moving patiently forward in waves. Even after several hundred listens I never know quite where it is going. But I always know that it is going somewhere, and that its final destination will feel like home.

•

A few hundred years ago, sentences were much more shackled together than now. They would begin with a *whereof* or a *howsobeit*, to show that they were resuming an unfinished thought. And they would use lots of conjunctive adverbs, those words that show how clauses link up—by, for instance, contrasting (*however*), adding (*moreover*), illustrating (*namely*) or proving (*therefore*). These adverbs are in long retreat. The use of *indeed* peaked in print in the eighteenth century and has been declining ever since. The number of *howevers* and *moreovers* has been falling since the 1840s. Readers today link sentences in their heads without lots of *thuses* and *whereupons* to do it for them.

One kind of prose still clings to the conjunctive adverb: academic writing, and the forms that mimic it, such as the school and student essay. This writing connects itself up carefully with proofs, examples, exceptions, nuances, finessings and equivocations. All those *of courses* and *admittedlys* and *to be sures* are there to inoculate the writer against the shameful disease of naivety. Often such writing is just too watertight, too neurotic about purging itself of inconsistencies. Rather like sealing a boat's hull with black tar, making prose unsinkable makes it ugly. It has sold its life and voice in return for that dubious virtue, invulnerability.

Using too many conjunctive adverbs suggests that you don't trust your reader to follow the native weave of your thought. Or you think that she doesn't trust you, and that without all this qualifying and exemplifying she will be picking endless holes in what you say. Both these fears get in the way of the ideal of writing—as a gift from writer to reader, the gift of telling someone what you know or have seen. Conjunctive adverb blight occurs when you worry that this is not enough, and revert to the classroom mode of writing for teacher, explaining what you half-know to someone who knows it better. So you shove in timorous caveats that all mean the same thing: *Is this what you wanted me to say?* These clog up the flow like wet hair in a plughole.

Conjunctive adverbs add more words to the sentence, all of which the reader needs to read. Thoreau called it "preponderating paste." Likewise, the meta-comment that scholarly writing deploys, such as *in this study I want to argue that* and *my contention is that* and *suffice it to conclude that,* slams the brake pedal on prose. People who write *it is to this question that we now turn* think they are helping the reader, but they are just giving her more words to read. Strangely, signposts work best when they are half-invisible, leading the reader on without advertising themselves. Transitions do their job well when they don't read like transitions, when they are more like those tongue-and-groove joints that make a single flat surface with the join hidden underneath.

You don't need gummy adverbs if you can join sentences just by drawing on tacit assumptions that writer and reader share about the world. Two sentences might be linked only by the common knowledge that car windshields frost over on cold nights, and that drivers run their engines as they scrape them clear. *That winter was the coldest I could recall. Each morning on my street I heard the ritual scraping of car windows while the engines idled.* Single sentences draw on such shared notions to make sense; sentences strung together are no different.

Here is the real risk posed by the computer. It doesn't so much destroy flow in writing as make it easier for you to fabricate it. It invites you to write your notes hugger-mugger on the screen and then fix them together with an armamentarium of linking *thuses* and *therefores*. The adverbs offer sham coherence, patching together sentences unlinked by patient thought. *For example* can feel tacked on to the previous sentence, merely adding rather than driving forward. *To name but two*, which writers resort to when they feel they have used too many *for examples*, implies that they could name more but really means that they can only name two. *Moreover* and *furthermore* are Columbo adverbs: all they mean is *and one more thing*, when the reader has already spotted that you've said one thing and are now saying something else. *Strikingly* or *tellingly* (or, worse, *it is no accident that*) are weak glue because something truly striking needs no buildup. Try cutting these words and see if the gist survives. It usually does.

A reader who needs to rely on conjunctive adverbs and other linking matter to guide her through a piece of prose is flying a plane in fog. In clear weather, you can fly a plane using only visual cues from the world outside the cockpit. By looking at the horizon you keep the plane level and straight (*orientation*). By looking at bits of the landscape, like rivers, roads and runways, you steer the plane to its destination (*navigation*). And by looking out for obstacles, like other planes, mountains and the ground, you avoid hitting things (*separation*). But if you can't see through the cockpit window, you have to abandon all this and fly the plane with just the instrument panel. Instrument flying is hard to learn and even harder to enjoy, and it means you are allowed to fly only predefined routes. Pilots call it being *in the soup*.

If, when reading a piece of writing, you can understand the words and the order they are in, but can't really see ahead of you, then you are instrument flying. You can get by. You know what the words, and the adverbial glue that links them up, mean. But you can't feel the writing move forward. You are in the soup. How much better not to have to keep checking your instruments but to fly in cloudless skies, relying on data supplied by your senses and seeing the sentences fold out in front of you as if you were just pointing your plane at the horizon.

•

Have faith in the reader. Do not underestimate her ability to assume an innate unity in a group of sentences and to follow unaided the unfolding thought. Where she needs help, light connectives such as *yet, so* and *still* will link up thoughts just as well as heavier ones like *however, therefore* and *nevertheless. What's more* and *then again* do the same job as *in addition* and *on the other hand* but with fewer syllables.

But is confusing when overused, especially if it comes twice in the same sentence, as the reader has to keep up with the handbrake turns of thought. *But* can often be cut, because the substance of the sentence makes the qualification clear enough. But using *but* to start a sentence is, whatever anyone else says, fine. It is short, sure-sounding and often clearer than an about-turn *however* halfway in. Use *however* only when you want to stress the word or phrase that precedes it. *I, however, prefer the word "but."*

Richard Hugo compares signposts in writing to that stock subtitle in silent movie westerns, *Meanwhile, back at the ranch ...* The words became an industry joke because they were superfluous. Overlaid on a shot of the ranch, they told the audience something it already knew. The same applies, Hugo writes, to *meanwhile* or *at the same time* in prose: it means that two things you mention together are happening at the same time, which is probably true in any case. Just as cinemagoers have learned to see the implied continuity of time and space across the quick cuts of a film, so have readers learned to make a little cognitive jump between sentences. Writing's firmest cement comes not from gluey adverbs but from the rhythm and music of how the sentences are arranged. "It is impossible to write meaningless sequences," Hugo writes. "In the world of imagination, all things belong. If you take that on faith, you may be foolish, but foolish like a trout."

•

You have probably forgotten by now that your reader is lost. She does not know the route to dry land across the sea-road of your thoughts. Why would she? If you do not know the way either, there is no hope and you are both sunk. But if you know the way too well, you may assume that the reader does, too, and she will sink while you sail blithely and uselessly on.

Guiding a reader through your sentences is a form of way-finding. In his 1960 book *The Image of the City*, the urban geographer Kevin Lynch calls wayfinding "a consistent use and organization of definite sensory cues from the external environment." Lynch argued that people are amazingly skilled at navigating their little patch of the world with only the barest of cues. Equatorial Africans use elephant paths to cross rainforests as easily as we cross cities. Aborigines walk the Australian outback using mnemonic "songlines" that can identify specific sand dunes or termite mounds. The Arctic Inuit find their way across wide bays by reading low clouds that reflect the earth below—those above soiled land-ice being dark and those above sea-ice white. Gauchos plot a route through the pampas by studying the direction of winds and the migration patterns of birds and other wild animals. Nowadays, admittedly, they are more likely to be riding with one arm in the air to get a better mobile signal.

The traditional explanation for how indigenous peoples found their way across apparently featureless landscapes was that they had a sixth sense, an intuition other people had lost. The explanation is patronizing to everyone. The truth is that all humans are natural wayfinders, solving complex spatial problems almost as easily as blinking. Only in the last few centuries have we begun to understand space mainly through instruments like compasses and the bird's-eye view we get from maps. Before then we were skilled at getting our cues from the world around us, at eye level—and, when deprived of these instruments, we still are.

People used to think that the thousands of far-flung islands in the Pacific were settled after being found accidentally by sailors drifting on rafts. The Pacific islanders knew different. Their oral traditions told them that their ancestors arrived on voyaging canoes, guided by skilled navigators, often sailing against the wind. In Hawaii, in 1973, a group of mariners and anthropologists decided to test this theory by forming the Polynesian Voyaging Society. They built a beautiful, double-hulled canoe called *Hokule'a*, or *Star of Gladness*. Then they tracked down one of the very few traditional navigators left—Mau Piailug, from the tiny Micronesian island of Satawal—and persuaded him to sail the *Hokule'a* the 2,500 miles from Hawaii to Tahiti.

In the spring of 1976, Mau set off with his crew, with no compass, sextant or charts. He did not use latitude, longitude or math of any kind. All he did was point the boat in the right slant of wind and along a line between a rising star and a setting one. He could read the ocean swells, detect shallower water by color, look for birds homing in the evening, and see the light from islands reflected on the underside of clouds, even identify the island from its reflection's shape. After just thirty-three days they made it to Tahiti, with half the island's people cheering them into harbor. Mau's voyage transformed the self-image of Pacific islanders, by showing that their homelands were settled through skilled seacraft. As Mau said, "If you can read the ocean, you'll never be lost."

Kevin Lynch thought that towns and cities should be legible like this—easy to read as we sail through them, using the clues given for free by our senses. His book greatly influenced architects and planners as they tried to help people find their way round streets, shopping malls, museums and art galleries. The first thing they did was to cut down on signs and other visual clutter. And then they tried to guide people through a place by drawing on their intuitions, their innate ability to read the world using clear landmarks, uninterrupted sightlines and coherent design.

The lesson for the sentence writer is that too much signposting may be as bad as too little. The reader does not need a master plan to follow or a map on which to plot a course before setting out. A journey through a text can be a line of stepping stones, to be crossed one at a time, just by putting one foot in front of the other.

Medieval scholars had a term for this kind of reading as the guided voyage of a thinking mind through the topography of the text: *ductus*. The word is still used today by palaeographers (decipherers of old handwriting) to mean a scribe's natural, unbroken stroke. But in the Middle Ages it referred to the reader's flowing journey through a piece of writing. Sometimes the writer wanted his reader to move quickly along with no obstacles, like water flowing through an aqueduct; sometimes he wanted him to work harder, or to stop and look around. Either way, the words were meant to lead the reader on, step by step.

True flow in writing is like this: a gradual unveiling, like pointing a boat, a wandering bark, at a star and seeing where it leads. You just need to be able to see the horizon and know your next move. Learn to read the ocean and you'll never be lost.

•

In the field of design, the same spirit now rules. The design critic Donald Norman calls it "natural mapping." Norman's work looks at why everyday things like washing machines and remote controls are so difficult to use. The culprit is the same one that makes a lot of writing hard to navigate: overengineering. For Norman, objects need clear *affordances*: the things that show us how to use them, like handles, grips and switches.

A door handle that needs to explain itself with a sign saying *push* or *pull* is just a bad design. The handle should tell us, wordlessly, whether to push or pull—with a push plate, or a hand-shaped hollow to fit your fingers in and pull. Car door handles, with indentations that afford entrance by the hand, are exemplary. So are salt and pepper cellars with transparent casings, which mean we do not waste precious moments checking the number of holes in the top and remembering what they mean. So is a felt-tip with a ribbed side, a clue to grip it there so it writes better.

In the 1990s Norman worked for Hewlett-Packard and Apple. He wrote *The Invisible Computer*, a book which claimed that computers were too hard to use and should fit more easily into our lives. Making a computer easy to use is difficult because, unlike a car door or a salt cellar, it does many things. And the computer industry keeps adding to these functions because it relies on generating sales through upgrades. A computer afflicted with featuritis slows the user down with useless trickery, like a sentence encumbered with needless intensifiers.

The best technology, Norman writes, is so buried we forget it is there. In the early days of motoring, just starting a car was a huge task. You had to prime the fuel, set the choke, open the throttle, then get out of the car and crank it up by hand. These days the engine hides under a hardly-ever-opened hood and most drivers give it no thought at all.

For Norman, a computer's workings should be as invisible as a car's engine and as instinctual to use. The most successful computer designs have followed his advice. I never joined the cult of Apple—with its audience-whooping product launches, its high-fiving early morning queues for the new iPhone, its mass sharing of the inspirational thoughts of its founder. But I do see why others fall so hard. Apple makes things that look so simple, you know how to use them in an instant. They solve problems you cannot see, so clean and elegant are the solutions. Their beauty is a side effect of their union of form and function, the way they so perfectly embody the point of their existence.

The cult of Apple truly began in 1998 with the iMac—its monitor and circuit board housed together in a single pod, as curvy and translucent as a Rowenta iron and as easy to use. No floppy drive or knotted cables: just USB ports, with all the connections hidden behind a neat door on the side—easier to get at than at the back—so you did not get tangled up in the usual wire linguine. All you had to do was plug it in and you were good to go.

Apple products drew on the natural ballet of human gestures to make them work. The iPod fit snugly in your palm, like a cigarette packet for those addicted to music instead of nicotine. It let you access a thousand songs in just a few spins and clicks of its scroll wheel, which looked like a stereo speaker, subtly hinting that this device was all about the music.

Then came the iPhone, at a time when everyone thought that BlackBerry-style mini-keyboards and styluses were the future. Instead the iPhone's multi-touch screen used that excellent pointing and prodding device, the finger, and that happy result of human evolution, the opposable thumb. The multi-touch screen turns us into cyborgs, blends of human and machine. Our fingers and thumbs perform sorcery, flicking through photos, zooming in on maps and turning pages with motions as easy as picking lint off a jacket or brushing dust off a book.

As for the iPad, a three-year-old can use it. Its chamfered corners let you scoop it up easily and swipe it into action, like a massive iPhone for people with clumsy fingers and poor motor coordination. In the Apple stores, with their grand entrances and light-filled naves, the true believers, or Macolytes, come to worship at the altar of the techno-faith. But for all the aura that these devices give off when new, what is truly beautiful about them is that after a while you use them with a shrug.

When I am trying to knit sentences together, I think of these arts of wayfinding and natural mapping and see if I can emulate them. I want my sentences to flow as if the reader were walking through a townscape with no need of a street map, or gliding through a series of doors in a long corridor without having to look whether to push or pull, or scooping up a tablet, prodding it and swiping it in one unthinking action. The best sentence design is like all good design: its elegant obviousness is a kind of unspoken poetry. Beautiful things have a built-in lucidity, and when something works well it is beautiful anyway. As Eric Gill put it, "Beauty looks after herself."

•

Beauty may look after herself, but flow in writing does not. Flow should *feel* natural but almost never *is*. It arrives only after the way has been carefully cleared and paved. Flowing sentences are forward-facing, drawing what they need from the previous sentence and then setting up the next one. The classic subject–predicate order starts with something known and adds something new, which the next sentence then starts with as something known. This echoes the familiar seesaw rhythm of spoken English, which refers to the information given in the previous phrase before saying something fresh. If each sentence moves the reader from where they were to somewhere else, it rarely needs any other connective padding.

But writing rarely comes out like this on the first go. It breaks the given-then-new rule and starts a sentence with a new idea, or an idea mentioned at the start, not the end, of the previous sentence, so that your reader has no setting for the idea. Since she assumes that sentences cohere by moving from old to new, she will try in vain to link it to the end of the previous sentence. She won't be lost, exactly, just a little thrown. Often all you need to do is tweak the sentence to put the old information at the front and the new at the end. The maligned passive voice may help, by letting you move words easily around. Inverting the usual subject–verb order also moves old information to the start. *On such subtle inversions* can the unity of our writing hang.

Making sentences cohere is fiddly like this. One especially nettlesome sentence-cohering task never goes away. You must help the reader keep track of something mentioned more than once across a run of sentences. How do you reword that thing to avoid awkward-sounding repetition, without the rewording itself sounding awkward?

As with all sentence cohesion, rewording works best when it is invisible. Sometimes you just need to switch from an indefinite to a definite article, to show you have mentioned something already. *I bought a boat. The boat had a leak.* Or you can call on those most useful English words, pronouns. The shorter and commoner a word, the less clunky it is to repeat it. An almost invisible word like *said* can be endlessly reused. Pronouns, too, are short and common and can be repeated ad infinitum with no ill effects.

The problem with pronouns is that their related noun is not always clear. Pointing pronouns like *this, these* and *here* can refer to already mentioned things without drawing attention to themselves—but the reader needs to know what *this* or *these* are, and where *here* is. When you rename something hitherto named, the word you are referring back to is the *antecedent* and the word that replaces it is the *anaphor*. The reader must be able to hold the antecedent in his head for long enough to link it to the anaphor, and without confusing it with other nearby words. The longer the sentence, the more likely that *it* or *they* or *she* could refer to more than one noun. If you can't vary the wording without keeping the antecedent clear, just abandon the rewording and repeat the word.

•

All noun variation comes down to pronouns. When a new noun sits in for an already mentioned noun, it should be a pronoun or what Steven Pinker calls a "pseudo-pronoun." That is, it should be more generic than the noun but still call it quickly to mind. Nominalizations can clog up sentences with nouniness, but they can also be handy pseudo-pronouns if you want to mention something a second time. When the bird started speaking I was *astonished*. That it spoke in Greek compounded my *astonishment*.

A hypernym, which is a more general word than its related hyponym, is usefully pronounish. *Bird* is a hypernym of the hyponym *swallow*, *flower* of *rose*, *dog* of *Labrador*. Hypernyms are handy for second mentions, so, for instance, *abalone* might become *the weird-looking molluscs that must be beaten with a hammer to make them tender enough to eat*. But then abalone clearly belong to the mollusc family. Most words do not fall into such neat pecking orders, because the world does not arrange itself so. The same word might be a hyponym of several hypernyms: *knife* might be one of *tool*, or *weapon*, or *cutlery*.

Pierre Roget's famous thesaurus tried to solve this problem and failed. Roget was inspired by Carl Linnaeus, the Swedish naturalist who classified every plant and animal into genus and species. He thought that a similar order could be brought to the unruly world of words, that these could be divided like flora and fauna into nicely tabulated categories. He devised core classes like "Abstract relations," "Space" and "Matter" and then subdivided them. *"Existence,"* the book begins. *"Existence*, being, entity; absolute being, the absolute ... *divineness* ..." Every word knows its place in creation: *indifference* sits between *aversion* and *desire*. Except that feelings cannot really be slotted neatly into grids like this. Indifference is its own state, not the midpoint between two extremes. If emotional states had to be classified like gastropods, the taxonomists' arguments would never end.

This is the problem with sentences written with a thesaurus too readily to hand. Words can be inserted into a sentence with no thought as to how they sit within it. A sentence is not a Linnaean hierarchy of words; it is an ecosystem. All the elements of an ecosystem—soil nutrients, plants, herbivores, carnivores—interact to form an equilibrium that is threatened if one part of it is disturbed. A sentence, too, is an organic community and changing one word can shift its delicate balance so that the whole thing feels disarranged, knocked out of kilter. It is like replacing a single note in a musical phrase with another and hoping the tune will still work. A sentence is a company of words, not a series of slots to be filled by stand-ins. Alter one word and you alter it all. A bad sentence can never be saved by swapping words; better throw it out and start again.

The lexicographer Henry Fowler called the labored racking up of synonyms "elegant variation." Driven on by an extreme fear of repetition, elegant variers only leave the reader feeling distracted and confused. The *Guardian* calls such synonyms "popular orange vegetables," or "povs," after one of its subeditors saw a report that used this phrase to avoid repeating *carrot*. Elegant variers are especially drawn to adjective–noun combos, such as *the furry forecaster* (the groundhog) or *the white stuff* (snow). Often the simple antidote is that self-effacing pronoun to which elegant variers seem allergic: *it*.

Elegant variants work when they add detail and color—when they do not just elegantly vary but move the writing along. When Nigel Slater elegantly varies *pasta* as "tender yet substantial ribbons of starch," it works because it says something new. The pasta has become a delicious incarnation of an energy source, just as a stick of cotton candy is a pink tuft of spun sugar, or a nut is a compacted pellet of protein, or a packet of butter is a cuboid of fat, a polyhedron of future flab on your thighs, giftwrapped in golden foil.

•

In this game of trying not to repeat the noun, pronouns are better than hypernyms, hypernyms are better than synonyms, synonyms are better than elegant variation, and elegant variation that adds information is better than elegant variation that just elegantly varies. But more often than you think, it is best just to repeat the noun.

How much a writer tolerates repetition comprises a key part of his voice. David Foster Wallace declared himself a "fiend" for elegant variation and having "alternative constructions at your fingertips." David Peace, at the other extreme, deploys inelegant repetition as an incantatory device. His novel *Red or Dead* records every match in which Bill Shankly managed Liverpool: "In September, 1960, Liverpool Football Club beat Scunthorpe United and they beat Leyton Orient. In October, 1960, Liverpool Football Club beat Derby County and they beat Lincoln City ..."

Most sports writers mask this repetitive side of sport—in which the same finite pool of people achieve infinite iterations of the same outcomes (goals, tries, points)—with elegant variations like "the goal-starved striker" or "the unsettled defender." Peace is not playing ball. Sport for him is just one thing after another, tedium and tension combined. His repetitions suggest a manager's life moving through the same joyless groove, every game a fresh slog.

Inept writers repeat words all over the place—a sure sign that they are using them in heedless, scattergun ways. But many capable writers vary words too much, unaware that the reader can live with quite a lot of repetition. They also over-vary their sentence structures. They know the basic rules of parallelism *within* sentences—that elements in a series, for instance, should be put in grammatically identical form. But they rarely use parallelism *between* sentences, missing the chance to show, via syntactical echoes and matching phrases, how they link up.

Readers find these symmetries helpful because they add coherence—which is not the same thing as cohesion. Cohesion is how a sentence interlaces with the next one, by ending in a way that allows the next one to begin. Coherence is how the reader gets an overall sense of what a group of sentences is about. Coherent sentences don't just link up like a daisy chain, each stalk slit and threaded to the next in line; they have an overarching order. A group of sentences needs both cohesion and coherence if the reader is to feel that the words belong together.

Skilled writers make a group of sentences cohere by starting them with the same subject. If they are writing about Jaffa cakes, then the subject of all the sentences will be *Jaffa cakes*. They might mix it up a bit by using pronouns or pronounish words so as not to start every sentence with *Jaffa cakes*. Or they might begin with a brief adverbial (*Surprisingly, Jaffa cakes make good tea-dunkers*) or prepositional phrase (*In size and shape, the Jaffa cake is really a biscuit*) to break up the monotony. But Jaffa cakes will still be the subject of every sentence. Perhaps you think this will sound monotonous and the reader will be sick of all these mentions of *Jaffa cakes*. But she will be too focused on what is being said about Jaffa cakes to be bothered by the repetition of *Jaffa cakes*.

As well as clarifying the writer's intent, such repetitions can be rhetorically powerful. That single repeated phrase, *Jaffa cakes*, might be all that is needed to hold the tune. The ancient art of rhetoric relies on linking ideas through these musical repetitions—by, for instance, starting each sentence with the same word (*anaphora*), or ending each sentence with the same word (*epistrophe*), or repeating the last word of one sentence as the first word of the next (*anadiplosis*). Alternating repetition with novelty gives writing its music, just as it gives music its magic. Repetition is fine if you and the reader know you are doing it. In this book, the word *sentence* appears over a thousand times.

•

Sentence length is another matter. Novice writers vary their sentence structure too much, but their sentence lengths too little. A good trick, when drafting a piece, is to press enter after every sentence, as if you were writing a poem and each full stop marked a line break. This renders the varied (or unvaried) lengths of your sentences instantly visible. And it foregrounds the full stop, reminding you of its power as the destination and final rest of each sentence. Winston Churchill wrote his speeches like this, in single-sentence lines, to more easily adjust his Augustan rhythms. If you keep pressing enter after every full stop, the music of your writing is easier to hear because now it can also be seen.

When you vary the length of your sentences, two things happen. First, as you fit your thoughts into shorter and longer forms, you come up with better wordings. Second, your writing will, as if by magic, fill with life and voice. Nicholas Tomalin, in his advice to neophyte journalists, pointed out that you got high marks for style if you just alternated long sentences with short ones. One of his teachers at Bryanston School, John Royds, had given him this tip when he became editor of the school magazine. Tomalin dispensed the advice casually, as if it were a weary hack's shortcut—and it is true that alternating short and long sentences sounds so easy that it should come across as a mere trick. But no. It works every time.

Virginia Woolf is known for her long, serpentine sentences, the clauses held loosely together with dashes, semicolons, parentheses and comma splices. Woolf wrote that she wanted to go beyond the "formal railway line of sentence," to show how people "feel or think or dream ... all over the place." She wanted to catch the butterfly restiveness of the human mind, and the evanescence of human life, as they came up against the seemingly solid surfaces of society and the world. But still, like almost every skilled writer, she starkly varies sentence length. Her long, elastic thought refrains are always colliding with shorter, percussive fragments.

In a letter to Vita Sackville-West, Woolf wrote that prose style was all rhythm, that we feel "this wave in the mind, long before it makes words to fit it," and that if we get that right we can never use the wrong words. Writing gets much of its rhythm from its full stops—or, more precisely, its cadences. Cadence is used generally to mean the rising and falling rhythm of writing. But it has a more precise meaning. A cadence is what comes in writing, speech or music at the end of each phrase. In music, a phrase is the smallest unit able to make sense on its own. And it ends at this point of half repose, a cadence, where it feels as if the music has, just for a moment, arrived somewhere, usually back at the piece's tonal center. In speech, a cadence is the fall in pitch at a natural stopping point, the end of a phrase. The voice drops on the last three syllables: a descending tritone. The American poet Amy Lowell called the cadence a "rhythmic curve ... corresponding roughly to the necessity of breathing."

In writing we get the same drop in pitch, if sounded only in our heads: a death-reminding fall at the sentence's end. A falling cadence signals that the sentence, and the sentiment, are done. Varied sentence length makes for varied gaps between the full stops, which makes for varied cadences. This lets the writing breathe and move and sing. It also means that the stops, the little deaths, seem natural because they arrive regularly but not too regularly. Before antilock braking systems, drivers had to learn *cadence braking*: repeatedly applying and releasing the brake so as to slow a skidding car without locking the steering. Skillfully applied cadences do the same to prose. They stop it skidding and jumping around, making the ride feel smooth and the braking easy and gradual.

Short and long sentences do different things. Short sentences make key points or recap them, and trade in swift action, jokes and little swerves in thought. Long ones take readers on a mental tour, offer a rambling inventory or knead and stretch out a thought like a pizza chef working dough. Short sentences give your brain a rest; long ones give it an aerobic workout. Short sentences imply that the world is cut and dried; long ones restore its ragged edges. Short sentences are declarative and sure; long ones are conditional and conjectural. Vary your sentence length and you mirror the way the mind works, veering between seductive certainty and hard-won nuance.

•

A group of sentences of varied lengths is called a paragraph. That is as good a definition of a paragraph as any, since no definition quite works. Most linguists see the sentence, or the clause, as the basic unit of prose and do not even bother to define a paragraph. A sentence must obey grammatical rules, but a paragraph need obey no rules. A sentence is infinitely variable in its ordering of words, but one paragraph varies from the next only in its length. Paragraphs are little more than their recalcitrant contents: sentences. Paragraphing is not a rulebook to be learned by rote so much as a knack to be acquired, a gradual tutoring of the eye and ear.

The paragraph belongs to the age of print. Before the printing press there were no paragraphs, although sentences were often divided into groups using some kind of inline typographic marker, like the fleuron or pilcrow. But these marks were fitfully deployed. The arrival of the printed book, and of English prose as a grown-up form, encouraged the use of paragraphs to dispel the monotony of blocks of type.

E. H. Lewis, in his 1894 book *A History of the English Paragraph*, says that the first "tolerable paragrapher" was William Tyndale. Tyndale wrote for an unschooled audience, so he used short sentences and short paragraphs. Those still writing in Latin or Latinate English saw the long, periodic sentence, around which many clauses could group, as the main unit of prose. But as English prose pulled loose from its Latin models, even the last-ditch Latinists came to see that not everything could fit in one sentence. So paragraphs began to do what had once been the work of long sentences: bringing clauses together to make meaningful music. They came into being when writers saw that a sentence could not be endless and include everything.

The Victorian educationalist Alexander Bain saw the paragraph as "a collection of sentences with unity of purpose." Bain's idea of the paragraph as a single developed thought came to rule over the school lesson and composition class. Students were taught that a paragraph should have a topic sentence stating the main idea, supporting sentences that amplified that idea, and a wrap-up sentence revisiting the idea. George Gopen calls this the *Wizard of Oz* paragraph, with its middle three sentences chanting *because, because, because*. The trouble with this sort of paragraph is that its life is over by the first sentence and the others are just there to write its obituary. The paragraph's entire story was foretold, its topic baited and primed from the start.

Skilled writers ignore all this. They use pure topic sentences rarely and wrap-up sentences hardly ever. In the first paragraph of a piece, they will often put the main point at the end, so the reader can feel out the writer's voice before finding out what the beef is. *I suppose you're wondering why I've brought you here*, that delayed drop is saying, then it tells them. Skilled writers will also often put the point of the final paragraph at its end, bringing the piece to a rounded close. If they do start a paragraph with a topic sentence, the other sentences will be a loose-limbed pirouette around the topic, not a series of hard proofs to support it.

Mostly, though, their paragraphs just evolve, creating anticipation with each passing sentence. The paragraph has a rough shape but that does not kill its potential to reveal and surprise. It is not self-contained, closed off from its neighboring paragraphs by the topic and wrap-up sentences that top and tail it. Instead it moves into the next paragraph with the reader barely noticing, as if the writer is a storyteller who has just paused briefly, to swallow some phlegm or recross his legs, and carried on with the tale.

Writing to Thomas Carlyle in 1838, Ralph Waldo Emerson described his own paragraphs as masses of "infinitely repellent particles." He assembled his essays bit by bit, from lone sentences in his journals. His paragraphs get their vitality, and their lucidity, from the varied length and makeup of the sentences rather than any affected order or connectedness. I am fairly sure he never wrote a topic sentence in his life. And yet he wrote wonderful paragraphs because each sentence in them is worth reading, and he amassed them in ways that made oddly compelling and persuasive shapes. Emerson knew that a paragraph is as much rhythm as argument, that the rhythm is itself the argument.

A paragraph, like a sentence, is a unit of sound as much as sense. It often starts with a short sentence—something simple like *There's a catch* or *Here's the rub*. (*To be* sentences are common paragraph openers.) Slightly less often, but still quite often, it will end with a short sentence. A short sentence may sit somewhere in the paragraph's middle, as a fresh assertion or a way of stopping the thought and sending it spinning in another direction, rather like the turn, or *volta*, in the ninth line of a sonnet. Longer sentences sit in between. Out of all this variety comes music. A paragraph brings together sentences of different lengths and shapes to make prose sing.

Gertrude Stein, listening to her beloved white poodle, Basket, drinking water from her bowl, said: "Paragraphs are emotional and sentences are not." She did not explain what she meant, but here is my theory. A dog slurping up water has a special rhythm. Unlike us it cannot just tip the water down its throat, nor suck it up, because it has hardly any suction in its cheeks. So it has to defeat gravity by lapping quickly with its tongue curled into a ladle shape, forcing the water into a column that can be chomped on and swallowed. This takes a lot of effort and the dog needs to take irregular breaks. I wonder if listening to Basket drinking, then stopping, then drinking again, reminded Stein of a paragraph's cadences, the different distances between the full stops. Paragraphs are emotional because they are about pace and variety as much as meaning and logic.

•

The paragraph is also visual—and the reader sees it before she reads it. What she sees, at a glance, is a silhouette of the writer's thoughts. Look at a printed page from the other side of a room. The words are a gray, illegible blur but the paragraphs, with their truncated first and last lines, can still be made out. A paragraph-free page is a lumpen slab of type and looks, however wonderful the writing might be, unenticing.

White space is welcoming. It breaks up the page, gives the words air and light and ushers the reader in. By some unfathomable alchemy, writing that looks good on the page, with none of the paragraphs too long or puddingy-looking, has a habit of also reading well. When writing on a computer, I indent my margins deeply so I can see how the paragraphs will look to a reader (because books have fewer words per line than a screen). Those that look right stand a better chance of reading right.

Just like sentences, paragraphs have shrunk. From the fifteenth century to the turn of the twentieth, the average paragraph length stayed steady at about 300 words. Then, under the influence of newsprint, they got shorter. The thin columns of newspapers needed shorter paragraphs to break up the text into unforbidding chunks.

The influence of advertising copy shortened the paragraph still further. Copywriting is all about the paragraphing, and it is worth any writer knowing a few copywriter's tricks. This is how I learned, as a boy, the visual power of paragraphs—by reading the full-page ads in the Sunday color supplements for things like Flymo hover mowers, Thomson holidays and Vesta Paella ("Little Costa and a lot of Brava"). I happened to be growing up in a golden age of long ad copy and I was drawn, without knowing how and why until much later, to its flair for making words move along the page.

The age of long copy began in 1959, with a famous ad produced by Bill Bernbach's agency in New York for Volkswagen: *Think Small*. The work of copywriter Julian Koenig and art director Helmut Krone, it had a photograph of a Beetle car, about the size of a coin, pictured at a slight angle, off-center, on a mostly white page. Beneath it were easy-to-read blocks of copy, written in what became the industry's signature voice: witty, intimate, conversational. Back then, car ads stressed size, speed and chrome-coated glamour. But this one all but conceded that Beetles were small and ugly, while cannily hinting that their drivers were too cool to care. It broke with the pummeled tone of traditional copy and the ad man Rosser Reeves's rule: "Tell 'em what ya gonna tell 'em, tell 'em, tell 'em what ya told 'em, and then do it again."

Aldous Huxley, who once worked in advertising, thought it easier to write ten decent sonnets than one good advertisement. Copywriting has to read smoothly or the reader will stop reading. To see what they were up against, apprentice copywriters were told to go to a railway station and watch the waiting passengers flicking resignedly through magazines. No one buys a magazine for the adverts, so an ad writer's readers are uniquely hard to hook. They cannot be pulled in by the usual compelling topics: gossip, politics, profanity, sex, death. They can be held only by a sure and steady voice.

The style of ad copy should be clear but also a little cool and oblique, implying a smartness just beyond the reader's reach. The tone should be irreverent, disarming, self-deprecating— and yet avoid being too much of any of these, so as not to grate. The writing should work like a charm, which means the charm must be buried. The sentences should feel springy and yet snap together like Legos. The last sentence should, like the end of a sonata, close the circle of meaning by coming back to the start.

The secret with all ad copy is flow. The starts of sentences and paragraphs are the pinch points where the writing may stall. The copywriter Paul Silverman once said that paragraph transitions were like the corners of a racetrack: the writer needed to fight the instinct to brake. Ad writers draw on a small arsenal of sentence beginnings, grabby ways of carrying readers forward, adding detail or changing tack. In adverts many sentences start with *and*, *but* and *or*. There are lots of confiding, parenthetical asides (but not too many to jar). Any unfamiliar or hard-to-pronounce word that could halt the reader is killed without mercy. Sentence length varies, for the cadences, but most sentences are still short. You can't get much shorter than *Think Small*: a verb and a flat adverb. Another of that ad's innovations was to put a full stop at the end of this two-word headline, making it not just a headline but a proper sentence, forcing the reader to pause at its end.

The prose must feel as if it is going somewhere. An old copywriter's trick is to write the start and finish and then fill in the middle. Imagine having to travel from your home to the nearest grocery store. Once you know where you are and where you are headed, you should be able to find the best route, because the start and end will recommend the streets in between.

•

The British ad writer David Abbott, revered in the business for his clean and agile copy, read his drafts aloud to himself in a mid-Atlantic lilt—a test that the sentences had just the right amount of schmaltz and just the right rhythm. The trick, he said, was to learn how to write a list so that it doesn't read like a list. The ad must give out the dull details, such as that Volkswagen Beetles are economical or easy to park, without it seeming as if they have been parachuted in. The parallelism that links sentences up through reverberating patterns does a much better job than "five reasons you should buy this thing."

This is good counsel for all writers, not just copywriters. The worst kinds of prose, like managerial blah, turn everything into a list. The sentences are just long lists of interchangeable clauses divided by semicolons. The arguments are bullet-pointed enumerations. The paragraphs are numbered hunks of text, split into sections and subsections, relieving the writer of the job of linking one lump of prose to the next. Reality is arranged consecutively but randomly. List-like writing is lifeless (listless?) because, unlike life, it has no natural beginning or end. In your head, what you want to say is probably also just a list. Make sure it doesn't come out as one, or at least try to camouflage it as a forward-rolling sequence.

In ad copy, the look of the paragraphs really matters. Until the 1960s copywriters wrote their copy and stuck it in an out-tray, from where it was whisked to the art directors in the studio and the writers never saw it again. Bill Bernbach was the first to put copywriters and art directors in the same room. They began working together on the look of the words—what the art directors called, disparagingly, *gray lines*. They started using clean, sans serif fonts and lots of white space to draw the reader in.

A poet, just like a copywriter, knows that this space—the blank strips of the inner and outer margins, the gutters at the top and bottom, the gaps between the lines—is what allows the blocks of words to exist. A sonnet, fourteen lines of ten syllables each, is an oblong block of type in the center of the page, bordered by silence. Our eyes collect data by registering light. The page's contrast of white and gray is the beginning of meaning, before we have even begun to decipher the words. Something only exists in relation to nothing. Unless the rest of the page is empty, the words cannot be read.

Architects think of a building not so much as walls, floors and ceilings but as the way that these enclose air, light and space. Actors and singers learn that a pause can carry as much meaning as the noise that breaks into it. The Japanese call this *ma*: the spatial void, or interval, that underpins their idea of artistic beauty. In the Eastern arts of flower arranging, Zen garden design and ink-wash painting, space is not there to be filled but to be preserved. Art draws its power from its silences, what gets left undrawn or unsaid. The empty space allows the elements in the piece to form lines that flow, drawing the viewer in and through it. Space is not background but emptiness full of potential.

Every typographer understands that the space between the type matters as much as the shape of the letters themselves. The letter-carver David Kindersley said that "a bad space is worse than a bad letter." How much of a gap you leave between the letters, between the words, between the lines, between the paragraphs: it all matters beyond words. Space makes the reader feel cared for, even if she can't put her finger on why. The way the writing looks is also what it says.

Paragraph writers take note. We hardly ever leave enough space between our words. We think that the reader will hang on our every phrase and forget that she is also a viewer, walking through the sculpted space of the page. The writer, just like an artist or architect, must offer a point of entry into the composition. Without it the words feel cluttered and inhospitable. Children's writers and illustrators know how vital is white space as a lure and an invitation, a promissory note to the child reader that she will not be bored. Adult readers never quite grow out of needing the same reassurance that they will not be interminably talked at. The writer Janice Galloway calls it "hauling the reader in," this use of white space "to make them do part of the work and bring the experiences that they have."

David Abbott would draft his copy in the column widths of the finished ad, so that he knew exactly how it would look. His ads began with a headline that commented on the picture as well as being the first sentence of the ad, like this one for a supermarket's wine selection: *At Sainsbury's, you can move from a house to a chateau for just £1.60.* This headline sentence led the reader, like a beckoning palm and a hand round the shoulder, into the rest. Abbott saw that writing was a visual art, a way of catching the eye and steering the gaze.

The age of long copy is over. Advertisers now assume that consumers, spoiled by television and the Internet, have no attention span for it. Ad copy has become short and arresting for the benefit of the time-poor and distracted. *Be inspired. Get connected. Think different.* But writers could still learn from those old ads about how to haul a reader in and make the writing flow. When David Abbott died, his fellow ad writer Robin Wight wrote that "his copy was easier to read than to ignore, so enticing was every next sentence." Isn't that what all writers should want: to make it easier to carry on reading than to stop?

•

Contemporary writers have fallen in love with white space. They are embracing the single-sentence paragraph, the block paragraph with white space above and below, and the section break marked by asterisks and other intervallic flourishes, or yet more white space. One sees it in the work of Lydia Davis, Annie Dillard, Vivian Gornick, Maggie Nelson, Sarah Manguso, David Shields and many others. The paragraph has become an island of words in the white sea of the page.

When Annie Dillard taught Maggie Nelson creative writing at Wesleyan University in the early 1990s, she advised her to "write a lot of short things and put them together." In *The Argonauts* Nelson tells the story of her relationship with her gender-fluid partner Harry Dodge using gaps and elisions, conveying the oddness of its course. One section begins, "And then, just like that, I was folding your son's laundry."

In *Swimming Studies*, the story of her teenage life as an Olympic swimming trialist for Canada, Leanne Shapton writes in a short-burst prose that fits her subject matter. It builds in slow increments, using the rhythms of training laps to disturb the linearity of a life. Shapton calls the book a "slide show of shuffling thoughts." This is how a mind works, she suggests, when the body is busy with repetitive actions and the view through one's goggles is fogged.

The obvious spur for this more elliptically linked writing is the Web. A new paragraph used to be marked in one way: indenting the first line. But when word processors arrived, block paragraphs, with a line space in between, became common. On the Internet the block paragraph reigns. Reading on a laptop or phone tires the eyes, and it is harder to keep your place. Line breaks help. Web writing needs its paragraphs to be stand-alone, skimmable and short.

Readers have gotten used to ellipses of thought between paragraphs, in the same way that they have learned to hop over the gaps between sentences without having their hands held. Perhaps this has something to do with the way we all now access and recycle words. With search engines and hypertext, we make our own way through the dizzying abundance of the Internet. We harvest data, then copy and paste the results. We ingest gobbet-like status updates and curate them into timelines, those ongoing, self-replenishing prose-poems on the everyday.

Like Gary Lutz's lonely sentences, the lonely paragraphs of contemporary writing are linked to each other by invisible causeways (rather as Don Paterson calls the stanza break a "connecting hallway"). They force the reader to make little intellectual and emotional jump cuts across the blank lines, unimpeded by pointers or markers. The sentences at the start and end of paragraphs carry special weight—just as, in a sentence, the start and end are the moments of greatest stress. Annie Dillard likes to begin or end her paragraphs by swerving into uncharted ground with some sudden question or statement such as "Why do we concern ourselves over which side of the membrane of soil our feet poke?" or "We are one of those animals, the ones whose neocortexes swelled, who just happen to write encyclopedias and fly to the moon." Sentences like this allow the reader to jump over the line space and feel that something has changed, even if he is not sure what. They are like soft landings that allow the writing to take off somewhere else entirely—the opposite of topic and wrap-up sentences, which seal a paragraph from its surroundings. The writing is alive, animate, moving forward to who knows where.

The word *paragraph* originally meant the paragraph break: it was the pause-providing mark (Greek: *graphos*) in the margin, beside (*para*) an unbroken block of text. The break is what matters, and the start and end of a paragraph are where it all happens. You can alter the whole tone of a sentence by moving it from the end of a paragraph to the start of a new one, and vice versa.

A paragraph break should nudge the writing along in some just-noticeable way while also offering, like a full stop, a pause for the reader. A neighbor of the writer Francine Prose once told her that he could not get on with Gabriel García Márquez's *The Autumn of the Patriarch* because he liked to drink while he was reading, and this paragraph-free (and nearly full-stop-free) novel gave him no clue as to when to have a sup of his beer. A writer can also use the paragraph break as a rest, a way of corralling her energies into spurts. Fay Weldon, a maestro of the two-sentence paragraph, told an interviewer that she writes in such short blocks because when she started writing her children were small, and "it was the most I could do to get three lines out between crises."

•

Like Lutzian lonely sentences, the lonely paragraphs of contemporary writing can teach us a couple of things about writing and flow, even if our own writing never goes to their elliptical extremes. The first thing is that what sticks their sentences together is voice—the sense of a mind, in Vivian Gornick's words, "puzzling its way out of its own shadows." However segmented or fragmentary the writing, it feels as if it has come from a single, navigating intelligence, embarking on an unmapped journey but making the words adhere through its voice.

Ander Monson compares this "lyric essay" form to the video game Katamari Damacy, in which a prince rolls a magic, adhesive ball around, collecting ever larger objects with it, until the ball grows large enough to consume the moon and stars. "The lyric essay," Monson writes, "is a super sticky power ball." The writer's voice is the adhesive force that picks up all the strands of fugitive information and makes them seem pertinent to each other and part of the same sticky ball.

Voice is the invisible force field, the holding energy that glues writing together. If it has no voice, no sense that the sentences all emerged from the same mind, then no amount of signposting or meta-comment will make it gel. But if it does have a voice, the reader will get used to glitches and quirks in the shape of its thought, rather as a neural network computer learns to work round the human idiosyncrasies of language. If it has a voice, the writing may be foolish, but it will be foolish like a trout. Voice is the elusive elixir of coherence.

The second thing this kind of writing teaches us is that a flowing voice comes through suggestive arrangement, not coercive connection. Evocative juxtaposition is as potent (and as hard to do well) as lockstep, linear argument. Maggie Nelson's *Bluets* is a seemingly formless reverie, in 240 numbered sections, on the color blue and its links with misery and heartbreak. But the thoughts that make up the book have, she writes, been "shuffled around countless times" and "made to appear, at long last, running forward as one river." The writing may look as shapeless and capricious as a list. But, like a Zen garden with hardly anything in it, it comes out of much patient, invisible work.

•

And so the cliché is true: writing is rewriting. A few fortunate writers say they feel the flow while writing. For most of us, writing never flows while we are doing it, and we must make do with rewriting to make it flow for the reader. Even the sentences we wrote quickly and sequentially in a fugue state of inspiration, in love with our own voice and its earth-shaking message to the world, will have to be cut up and rearranged.

(Especially those.) Only when we have hacked our sentences into a shape that is less than a mortifying mess can we see the hundred other things wrong with them. Only by putting the words into a semblance of order can we see how muddled they still are.

None of this should be surprising, given that a defining quality of writing, as compared to speaking, is that it can be withheld and redone. Writing *is* rewriting. And the rewriting begins with the paragraphs: conflating them, moving them round, testing the eye appeal of different lengths on the page. The paragraphs help you see which thoughts need to be developed and which compressed, where you need to linger and where you need to pick up the pace.

Wonky paragraphs are a helpful aesthetic enticement to revise. I get mildly exercised by one or two words left hanging in a line on their own at the end of a paragraph, rather as some people get exercised by slightly wonky pictures on walls. So I crop sentences to make the paragraph more like an oblong block. It is odd how this little visual incentive leads you to find cuttable words that might otherwise have been missed. Editing like this feels like sculpting: you chip away at a block of words until the shape looks right.

You will often find a hidden flow not by writing new words but just by deleting and rearranging. If you fix your efforts first on getting rid of what does not work, and moving around what is already there, you may unearth a buried coherence. Early drafts find you too wedded to set plans and trying to force the words together. Only an anemic link will get you from paragraph A to paragraph B and every other road seems blocked. But then you find that getting rid of paragraph B, or shunting it elsewhere, opens up a non-anemic link between paragraph A and paragraph C. A first draft is like a creaky stage musical, with lots of stilted dialogue exposition to fill the gaps between the songs and move the story on. While rewriting it you discover what you should have known all along, that you can just go straight from one song into another.

The sharp-eyed will have noticed the bad news sneaked in at the end there. You may have to delete entire paragraphs of your writing. Editing is best begun by lifting whole blocks from the work first, rather than trying to overcompress at sentence level. This is painful—there goes that bit I strove and wilted over—but it is the only way. Write in sentences, edit in paragraphs. Then start writing in sentences again.

Writing that flows is hard work made to look easy. Italians call it *sprezzatura*: studied carelessness. The word comes from Baldassare Castiglione's 1528 work *The Book of the Courtier*. Castiglione's (fictional) courtier defines it as "an easy facility in accomplishing difficult actions which hides the conscious effort that went into them." With *sprezzatura* the courtier avoids seeming calculating, a vital asset in a court awash with intrigue. Castiglione writes that a great painter, too, is blessed with this gift for creating "one single unlabored line, a single brushstroke, drawn with ease so that it seems that the hand moved without any effort or skill and reached its end all by itself." A writer's flow, like a painter's line, may hide a lifetime of effort behind its Potemkin village of effortlessness.

When the word *sprezzatura* migrated to England, the etiquette books misread it so it came to mean a certain kind of upper-class languor. But it is the skill hidden in *sprezzatura*, not the idleness, that counts. The reader's pleasure in flowing writing comes partly from knowing that the seeming spontaneity is rehearsed. Someone you do not know has cared enough about you to turn their lonely labor into something that falls well on the ears and fizzes with life for your benefit. All that effort has been shrunk into a form that surges through your brain like a fast car on an empty road. The writer built the road. She may have spent years hacking down trees and blasting hillsides to make a straight run. But the reader can be spared the dreary details. An old Gaelic blessing goes: "May the road rise up to meet you." We should wish our readers the same road through our sentences—as if the words were rising up to meet them, with the wind at their backs.

•

Flow, for your reader, means a state of fierce but happy concentration. The psychologist Mihaly Csikszentmihalyi says that this occurs when a person's mind and body are so immersed in a task that each stage runs seamlessly into the next. Flow is the optimal combination of muscle and nerve, of thought and feeling, effort and pleasure. A solo yachtsman feels flow when straining to hold a tight course, as his body works in tension and harmony with the wind, sail, waves and boat. A pianist is energized by the intricacy of a piece but also feels the fingers falling naturally on the right keys, so that motor memory kicks in. A free climber feels every new rock hold for the hands and feet appearing at just the right place and moment, and is absorbed in one task: reaching the top.

Flow is joyful, Csikszentmihalyi writes, because our minds crave order. Without order we are adrift in a meaningless world, with oblivion the only certain end. Humans are always "cheating chaos," making order out of the world's glorious confusion. For billions of years, fires on earth started only at random, from volcanoes, lightning or the sun's heat on shriveled leaves. Then early humans worked out how to start them on purpose, and to use them for heat and light. By ordering fire they learned to cook meat, clear land, burn waste, forge metal, light fuel and fight wars. With fire they changed the world forever.

Here is another way of cheating chaos: write a sentence, then another, then another. Somewhere deep in unrecorded time the human brain evolved an inner voice, but it was wandering and unruly. The invention of the sentence helped us shepherd that voice into sense and offer up its contents to others. It is still the best way we have of stuffing the world into the Procrustean bed of words.

Flow occurs when you are in pursuit of something that feels both worthwhile and just the right amount of difficult. There is a perfect fit between the challenge of a task and your capacity to complete it. Often we watch TV, or browse the Web, or scroll down a timeline, as a mild narcotic, an undemanding way of stopping us from daydreaming. But even the most pleasurable reading demands something of the reader. Writing flows when there is something for the eye and mind to chew on without it ever being a chore.

·

How do you know, since the act of writing hardly ever flows, that you have made your words flow for the reader? You don't. The finishing line can't be seen and, when you cross it, no klaxon sounds. It arrives, perhaps, when you turn into a reader of your own writing. You have put your sentences aside for a few days and come back to them when part of you has forgotten the worry that went into making them, forgotten even that it was you who wrote them. With luck, the links between your sentences no longer seem forced and contrived, even when the writing has involved a great deal of forcing and contriving. The flow seems to carry you along, over the dying falls of the full stops and the little leaps of the paragraph breaks, with the right-seeming blend of inevitability and revelation.

Yes, these words belong together. And their belongingness feels natural, even though they came very unflowingly out of your shambolic head. Now your actual reader just has to feel the same way about them—and that, of course, is up to her.

7.

A Small, Good Thing

Or why a sentence should be a gift to the world

Reading a sentence should never be a grim duty. This obdurate fact about writing stays true however much you scale it up. Most paragraphs are longer than they need to be, likewise most chapters. Most books go on for fifty pages longer than they should. We forget all this because it is less effort to speak than to listen. Writing is not a sermon, and at some point, sooner than we think, we should stop. No one is ever as interested as we are in what we have to say. They need to eat, or catch a train, or go to bed because they have work in the morning. The courteous actor says his lines and leaves the stage with no encore.

Just as a good sentence can be half out of control but must still feel as if it is moving toward resolution, so, too, with a book. Books, like sentences, create expectations about when they will end, and not only because of the dwindling number of pages that the reader can feel are left. The start of a final chapter is a promise to the reader that the writer will not detain him much longer. This book has moved from single words to short sentences, to long ones, to sentences joined together. And so now you have begun to exhale a final mental breath, as it seems to be coming toward its last full stop. But there are just a few things left to say—succinctly, so as not to try your patience when you are doing the readerly equivalent of putting on your coat.

I have said that a sentence is a gift. But it is an unusual kind of gift, given with little knowledge of the recipient, or any certainty that there will even be one. In one of his essays, Barry

Lopez calls a gift "the illiterate voice of the heart." A sentence is that kind of gift, even if in this case it is clearly best if the illiteracy is figurative. The gift comes from the illiterate heart because a sentence feels like the only way of saying what you have to say. And the gift is more precious because it is not neatly wrapped, tied with a ribbon bow and handed over to someone you know, but sent out into the world to be found. The desire to send out such a gift is remarkably resilient, as the following (brief) stories will show.

•

In May 1943 the neuropsychologist Aleksandr Luria received a new patient at his rehabilitation hospital at Kisegatch in the southern Urals. Lev Zazetsky was a twenty-three-year-old Russian sub lieutenant. At the Battle of Smolensk two months earlier, a German bullet had blown some of his brain away. Before the war he had been a star engineering student. Now his memory, vision and language were all shot to bits. He could barely talk and could only read by decrypting each syllable like a very young child. For the next twenty-six years Luria treated Zazetsky, as he fought to reclaim some of his old self.

The root of Zazetsky's problem was his failure to see syntax. The damage to his cerebral cortex meant that he could not fuse parts into a whole. All he could see was single words, not the meaning created by their arrangement. Sentences trading in comparisons, such as "Is a fly bigger than an elephant?," were beyond him. So were those in which the word order mashed up the temporal order, such as "I had breakfast after reading the newspaper." The only sentences he could read were as terse as a *Dick and Jane* book: "Winter came. It grew cold. Snow fell. The pond froze. The children went ice-skating."

Then Luria made a breakthrough. Zazetsky could write, just about, once he had been slowly retaught how to hold a pencil. Luria told him to stop worrying about forming discrete letters and to trust the natural motions of his hand, without lifting it from the paper. The words began to form into sentences. Luria called this automatic motor skill "kinetic melody." Kinetic melody was also there in the urge to sing, dance or run, all of which we do best when we do not overthink them.

This breakthrough changed Zazetsky's life. He could not understand what he heard on the radio, nor help round the house, nor go for a walk without getting lost. But he could write a journal, even if it was only a few sentences each day and this left him shattered. He kept at it, Luria felt, because writing was his main link with life. With syntax, he could pick up the pieces of his self and put it back together.

Over the next twenty-five years, Zazetsky wrote 3,000 pages—about a page every three days. His sentences may have been hard-won but they hummed with life. His inability to write outside of linear time made for its own penetrating clarity: "As for the flight of a bullet, or a shell or bomb fragment, that rips open a man's skull, splitting and burning the tissues of his brain, crippling his memory, sight, hearing, awareness—these days people don't find anything extraordinary in that. But if it's not extraordinary, why am I ill? Why doesn't my memory function, my sight return? Why does my head continually ache and buzz?"

In writing his journal this deeply debilitated man attained a kind of nobility. He had found a way, in Luria's words, "to live, not merely exist." Luria's book about him, *The Man with a Shattered World*, leaves him still living with his parents in his home town of Komovsk, sitting at his desk each morning, working on his journal. He died in 1993 at the age of seventy-three, still writing sentences to himself.

•

In 1992, at the age of sixty-nine, John Hale suffered a devastating stroke. The effects were similar to those Zazetsky experienced, and similarly paradoxical. *Stroke* is the most befitting of nouns for the assault on the brain that it names. It recalls both the word's other main senses, being both a painless caress from the hand of death and a clean slicing off of one's faculties, as if by a sharp blade. For Hale, losing nerve tissue in the brain wreaked havoc only randomly and incompletely. Some of his more complex abilities survived intact but the skeleton of logic that bore them was now a heap of broken bones.

Before his stroke he had been a professor at University College London, a renowned historian of the Renaissance and himself a renaissance man: a brilliant talker, teacher, scholar and writer. He had just completed his magnum opus, *The Civilization of Europe in the Renaissance*, a gigantic portrait of the age. He had loved writing ever since, as a young boy, he would compose little essays about his appendix operation or his uncle's false nose, kept in place with an elastic band after the real one had been blown off in a Somme trench. As a grown-up, Hale wrote in the evening, after a full day's teaching, in a fluent hand with barely a crossing out. All he needed for the words to flow was some desk space, a refill pad of lined paper, a cheap pen and a packet of cigarettes.

Within a year of the stroke he had regained much of his mobility. He could find his way round his beloved Venice unaided and was once again a familiar sight at art openings, pointing at paintings and gesticulating colorfully. In conversation he mostly just said "da woah," "ach" or "ohmygod." But his speech kept to its old rhythms and his friends were sure they understood him.

Writing was another matter. He regained a limited ability to write with his left hand, but could only produce stray words, sheared from sense and each other. Having mislaid the rules of syntax, he was baffled by questions that began with *who*, *what*, *when* or *where*. He could still insert the missing words in other people's sentences, scratch out the names of Renaissance painters, and compose brief, frantic declarations of love to his wife. At Christmas 1995 he managed a sentence: "I feel my writing returning." But it never did.

•

When you lose the ability to write them, sentences matter more than ever, and you will do anything to make them again. In the summer of 2008, at the age of sixty, the historian Tony Judt found himself hitting the wrong keys when he typed. That autumn he was diagnosed with Lou Gehrig's disease, a rare motor neurone condition, which was now destroying his body at speed. By the winter he could not use his hands and by the following spring he was in a wheelchair.

He could still speak but, even for someone as eloquent as Judt, that was not enough. He wanted to keep on writing. "The salient quality of this particular neurodegenerative disorder," he wrote, "is that it leaves your mind clear to reflect on the past, present and future, but steadily deprives you of any means of converting those reflections into words . . . For someone wishing to remain a communicator of words and concepts, this poses an unusual challenge."

Judt's answer to this challenge was to adapt the ancient mnemonic method of the "memory palace." Lying awake at night, his head buzzing with thoughts he could not write down, he pictured a Swiss ski chalet he had known as a boy. Then he put his thoughts in different rooms within it. He retained the power of speech, so in the morning was able to recover his thoughts from the chalet and, with the help of an amanuensis, turn them into writing.

He dictated two books and many essays like this, and delivered from memory his last lecture to his students at New York University. Before his illness he had seen himself "as a literary Gepetto, building little Pinocchios of assertion and evidence." Now his writing was less cerebral, instead drawing intuitively on the beat and pace of sentences crammed in his head from a lifetime's reading. For me these last pieces, completed before his death in 2010, are better written—more personal, allusive, musical—than anything else he wrote.

•

There is something heroic about this clinging so tenaciously to the act of writing. Most people live their whole lives without writing any more than they have to. Could Judt and the others not have admitted defeat and found an easier way to make themselves known to others? I doubt it. They were only doing what any writer does, after all: cussedly making sentences that no one asked for and no one will be obliged to read. And we carry on doing it even though most of us find dredging up words and deciding on their order to be slow work with unsocial hours.

We stick at it, I think, because a sentence allows us to sound like another version of ourselves. Most of the bad sentences I have written suffered from the same problem: I did not think that my own voice was worth hearing. I believed deep down that what I had to say was insufficiently interesting. So I coated my style with a blandly professional, voiceless veneer to make it resemble other, more respectable pieces of writing. Or I wrote in a contorted, fudging way that I thought would let me say the one tiny, specialized thing no one else had said, whether it happened to be interesting or not. I forgot that the whole point of a sentence is that it gives us a voice—one as unique and inimitable, we hope, as our actual voices, and able to stand in for them when we are not around.

In my case, this actual voice is one I have never liked. As a lecturer I know that it is, with the arguable exception of my brain, the most vital tool I have—as vital as dextrous fingers are to a pianist. But I have spent my whole career failing to get rid of the usual bad habits, like shallow breathing, dropped consonants and a falling inflection, that we acquire when we are unsure if others want to hear what we have to say. In front of a class my voice still has a habit of sinking into my throat or dying a rasping death. It leaves me feeling defeated and not up to my job— which, if I can't use my voice, I'm not.

An actual voice, unlike a written voice carefully worked on, can let us down. Any bit of tension in the shoulders, chest or abdomen, even locked knees or a sprained ankle, affects the sound that comes out of our mouths. Along the way into adulthood, we become estranged from our bodies and mislay the full potential of our voices. By releasing words half-heartedly into the space around us we leak evidence of our moods and our failings. A classic symptom of depression is dull vocal tone. That lump in the throat I get when I am very low feels as if my voice is lodged in my windpipe and I can neither release it nor gulp it down.

I wonder if people like me, whose voices in real life are so unreliable, are drawn to writing because it lets us rework our words until they fall well. We like the idea of letting sentences speak in our place. These sentences turn out to be brave and unflinching in ways that we are not. They come to stand in not just for our voices but for our gait, tread, gestures, shrugs and bodily tics—all the unsatisfactory ways we take up space in the world.

•

A written voice is not about putting your actual self (whoever that is) on the page. Sometimes I wish I were the person I sound like in these sentences, but I am not. If I seem sure in them, like someone who knows how to write a sentence, it is only because I do not much like writing clogged with qualifications and second thoughts. Forced to choose, I would rather sound clear than be right.

You acquire a written voice not when you learn to sound like yourself, but when you perfect the knack of slotting words together so that they sound like a convincing impression of a whole, consistent person. A written voice is a composite of your skill at selecting and arranging words and your genuine care for and commitment to what they are saying. That voice is not you, but it may be a buried, better-said version of you. It was lost amid your disheveled thoughts and wordless anxieties, until you pulled it out of yourself, as a flowing line of sentences.

Sounding like yourself, or at least the avatar of yourself that you have made out of words, is the only way to make others interested in what you have to say. Your voice gives whatever it is you want to say a home. When your writing has a voice, you are no longer cornering and badgering the reader with a jerry-built argument. Instead the argument arises out of the act of noticing something about the world from one tiny spot on it—the one occupied by the writer—and sharing it with the reader. This, it says, is what life looks like from here.

For those of us without a faith, the sentence feels, in some small way, devotional. It pays homage, not by thanking God for the world's existence but by thanking the world itself for existing. The thanking happens not by worshipping but by noticing. We are the only animals who are truly paying attention. No other living thing seems to be curious about things that they cannot mate with, play with, scrounge off or eat. We humans are the noticers. If our lives have any point, which I doubt, it might be this: to notice the world with our own eyes and to wrap that noticing in words. For this we made the perfect receptacle—a sentence.

"Everything that needs to be said has already been said," wrote André Gide. "But since no one was listening, everything must be said again." Our lives are an inventory of clichés. All of it has happened already to everyone else, for at least as long as people have written it all down. Toddler rages, family dramas, adolescent strops, asymmetrical fallings in and out of love, toxic friendships and enmities, worrying and delighting over children, thwarted or fudged ambitions, the slow-motion hurtle into aging and dying—and in between, snatched moments of laughter, enlightenment and joy. All very commonplace and predictable. But these clichés still have to be lived, and written about in a way that shows how *sui generis* they feel when they are. As Masha says in Chekhov's *The Three Sisters*, "we each have to solve our own lives." And, she might have added, we each have to write our own sentences.

So we should cherish what allows us to write them—arms,

hands, sight, motor skills and a memory—and use them while we may, for one day it will be otherwise. One day, perhaps sooner than we think, we will be beached up in the world, unable to write sentences anymore.

I don't look after my body well, but I do look after the parts of it I need to write. I stretch and squeeze my fingers, giving them miniature gym workouts, so I don't injure them from repetitive strain. My right shoulder and arm get stiff—an industrial injury I have heard called "mouse arm"—and so I knead them with a knobbly self-massage stick. Recalling with a wince the students of mine who could not write after breaking their writing arms, I try to keep my limbs in working order. If I ever trip over a loose paving stone, I must remember (being left-handed) to break my fall with my right arm. Like Sub Lieutenant Zazetsky, writing sentences is how I live, not merely exist.

•

Most accounts of that elusive state, happiness, include some sense of self-forgetting immersion, of feeling pleasantly enmeshed in the world. The poet Donald Hall calls it "absorbedness," a word he likes because it is "a noun with a lot of verb in it." Sometimes this sense of absorbedness is thwarted by a sort of blockage in our mental cisterns. We feel severed from the world and turn inward, running down our own, nonrenewable resources until we are empty and in despair.

In his book *Nature Cure* Richard Mabey writes about how, in his late fifties, he fell into a paralyzing depression that lasted nearly three years. All his life he had felt anchored by the return each May of the swifts, the last of our spring visitors, their aerial courtship displays and adolescent screeches announcing that summer was near. But when the depression descended, he stopped caring if they came back or not. He spent his days curled up in bed like a wounded animal, this anti-life of depression contrasting with the swift's unending vitality, its perpetual life on the wing. Eventually, his reawakened interest in the swifts signaled the lifting of his mood. Moving to a new landscape, in Norfolk's Waveney Valley, he reconnected with nature and began living again.

While I have been writing the 4,000 sentences in this book, I have failed to spot the swifts arriving, or any other migrating birds. The weather has blown hot and cold, the odd storm has ridden in from the west and the trees have morphed through the seasons, all of it unremarked upon by me. I have been like the five-year-old Robert in Edward St. Aubyn's *Mother's Milk*, "so caught up in building sentences that he has almost forgotten the barbaric days when thinking was like a splash of color landing on a page."

I have dimly noticed, while my world has narrowed to a computer screen, that a block of apartments has been rising up from waste ground over the road. Out of the corner of one eye I have clocked the hi-vis vested builders raising beams and bricking walls. Still it is a shock now to see bare earth become a building, with light in the odd window coming on at dusk. While I have been making flimsy things out of words, others have been making more concrete things out of concrete.

Meanwhile it feels as if the world is falling to pieces. Each day another ugly item on the news seems to peel away more of the thin coating of civilization that insulates us from the human genius for cruelty and self-harm. In response I have buried my head in the private sandpit of my desk. Like Thomas Hardy, I fear I may be chided by the moon for the "blinkered mind" that makes me want to write "in a world of such a kind." Or perhaps I will be accused as Flaubert's mother accused him: "Your mania for sentences has dried up your heart." At times like these, writing can feel like a poor substitute for being, an inward compulsion that cuts us off from the real.

And yet, as Richard Mabey eventually realizes, this distinction, between writing and life, is false. His depression was triggered—in the sense that depression is triggered by anything, which often it isn't—by his sense that his writing had amounted to nothing and had stopped him ever living a grown-up life. But he comes to see that writing is also life, a perfectly natural way of being—the "semi-permeable membrane," in fact, through which our species interacts with the non-human world. A writer, he decides, is as much a part of the world as a screeching swift.

For everyone is an equal citizen in the state of sentencehood. Sentences give us a shared space to find meaning in the world together. Like any form of human culture—breaking bread, making music, playing games—they bind us to each other and to the earth. They are where stranger talks to stranger in the silence of the page. Weaving words into this sense-making mesh is one way to fend off confusion and loneliness and give meaning to our lives. The familiar shape of a sentence reminds us that we are all on the same page, singing life's song in unison, grouping words into these little heaps of sense for as long as we live.

•

When I am coming out of a dispiriting mood, and feeling rejoined to the world, I don't start worrying about whether the swifts will ever return. I start thinking in sentences again. I notice the ones printed on railway platform signs, or the walls of train carriages, or bottles of pills, and roll them silently round my head. *Passing trains cause air turbulence. Please keep this seat available to those who may need it. If irritation occurs, discontinue use.*

As the words snap together they link me, in some small way, to the faceless person, the mute inglorious Milton, who wrote them. *This pencil is made with recycled CD cases.* I dislike the modern habit of removing articles from sentences in signs and so mentally reinsert them. *Do not place heavy items on [the] overhead luggage rack.* One sentence in a magazine ad I keep seeing—*Transform your existing staircase in just 48 hours*—has started to read like a question on an exam paper. Sentences are strange, and the closer and more carefully you read them, the stranger they seem.

I have learned to take this renewed interest in sentences as a sign that my mood is about to lift. The most reliable antidepressant is rekindled curiosity, and only the curious try to draw bits of the world together into words. The word *curious* derives from the Latin *cura*, which also gives us both *cure* and *care*. Curiosity is a cure for self-absorption, the cure being to care about the world and lay down roots in it again. Reading and writing sentences is a means of laying down these roots, of achieving *absorbedness*. And to be truly absorbed in anything is to be blessed.

•

My style guide by stealth seems to have turned into a love letter to the sentence—this thing that can make me feel as if I am talking into a void, but that has always, in the end, reunited me with the world. A muted love letter, perhaps, because a sentence's pleasures do not suit lavish avowals. They are low-key, ordinary, leveling. A sentence is a "small, good thing," like the warm cinnamon rolls the baker makes for the grieving parents in the Raymond Carver story of that name.

I am hoping that a love letter to a small, good thing will feel more useful to the reader than an English lesson. Even if I had anything to teach, it wouldn't matter. You only learn to write sentences by reading enough of them, and then writing enough of them, although the moment of "enough" never quite arrives. I knew I could only show you how to make sentences—how *I* make sentences—by making them and putting them in a book. A worry-making enterprise, for sure, since that book now has to stand and fall by its sentences. But doesn't that just make it like any book? So here they are, and here it is. These sentences, this book.

Twenty Sentences on Sentences

1. Listen, read and write for the sentences, because the sentence must be got right or nothing will be right.

2. A sentence is not about self-expression but about editing your thoughts into a partly feigned fluency, building a ladder of words up to a better self.

3. Train your ears, for how a sentence sounds in the head is also what it says to the heart.

4. The bones of a sentence are just a noun and a verb, so put the right nouns and verbs in the right slots and the other words fall into place around them.

5. Good prose is not a windowpane: a sentence reads best when the writer has tasted and relished the words, not tried to make them invisible.

6. Your sentences should mimic the naturalness of speech, so long as you remember that speech is not really natural and that writing is not really like speech.

7. Short words are best, for their clarity and chewy vowels, but the odd long word in a sentence draws just the right amount of attention to itself.

8. Verbal economy in a sentence is a virtue but an over-prized one: words are precious but they need to be spent.

9. Learn to love the full stop, and think of it as the goal toward which your words adamantly move—because a good sentence, like a good life, needs a good death.

10. If you keep the phrases short, and leave the longest phrase until last, the reader can cut a long sentence up into pieces in her head and swallow them whole.

11. Your sentences should sound slightly more naive than you are, for good writing is done with a cold eye but an open heart, and it is better to be always clear than always right.

12. The reader can live with more repetition—of both words and syntax—than you think, and these echoes within and between your sentences shed light on what you meant to say.

13. Vary the length of your sentences, and your words will be filled with life and music.

14. Because sentences have to live alongside each other, not all of them can dazzle the reader with their brilliance.

15. You can change the whole tone of a sentence by moving it from the end of a paragraph to the start of a new one, and vice versa.

16. Shorten your paragraphs: white space between sentences never fails to be welcoming.

17. A paragraph is not a single topic hammered home with proofs, but a rhythm made by the sentences rubbing up against each other, a rhythm which is itself the argument.

18. A reader needs no chaperone: signposting should be invisible and the sentences cohere through suggestive arrangement, not coercive connection.

19. Voice is the holding energy that glues sentences together, the elusive elixir of coherence that gives whatever it is you want to say a home.

20. A sentence is a gift from writer to reader, one that should never have to be bought—with boredom, confusion, the duty to admire the giver, or anything else.

Select Bibliography

Rather than weigh this book down with end matter, I have included only key texts here and have not referenced all quotations, such as those that are easily findable online or that have the sources mentioned alongside them in the text. To those who like every quote endnoted, I am sorry. I was you once. All the italicized sentences used as examples in the book are my own inventions, or are in common use, or their authors are clearly identified.

The books I have found most helpful while writing these sentences are Michael Billig's *Learn to Write Badly: How to Succeed in the Social Sciences* (Cambridge: Cambridge University Press, 2013); Peter Elbow's *Vernacular Eloquence: What Speech Can Bring to Writing* (New York: Oxford University Press, 2012); George Gopen's *The Sense of Structure: Writing from the Reader's Perspective* (New York: Pearson, 2004); Verlyn Klinkenborg's *Several Short Sentences About Writing* (New York: Vintage, 2013); Richard Lanham's *Style: An Anti-Textbook* (New Haven: Yale University Press, 1974); Francis Noël-Thomas and Mark Turner's *Clear and Simple as the Truth: Writing Classic Prose*, 2nd edn (Princeton: Princeton University Press, 2011); Virginia Tufte's *Artful Sentences: Syntax as Style* (Cheshire, CT: Graphics Press, 2006); and Joseph Williams's *Style: Ten Lessons in Clarity and Grace*, 5th edn (New York: Longman, 1997).

1. A Pedant's Apology

Hardy, G. H., *A Mathematician's Apology* (Cambridge: Cambridge University Press, 1992).

2. The Ape That Writes Sentences

Berry, Wendell, "Standing by Words," *Hudson Review* 33, 4 (1980–81): 489–521.

——, "Why I Am Not Going to Buy a Computer," in *The World-Ending Fire: The Essential Wendell Berry*, ed. Paul Kingsnorth (London: Allen Lane, 2017), pp. 236–43.

Carter, Angela, "Introduction," in Carter (ed.), *The Virago Book of Fairy Tales* (London: Virago, 1990), pp. ix–xxii.

Davie, Donald, *Articulate Energy: An Inquiry into the Syntax of English Poetry* (London: Routledge & Kegan Paul, 1955).

Finlay, Alec (ed.), *Ian Hamilton Finlay: Selections* (Berkeley: University of California Press, 2012).

Grubbs, Morris A., "A Practical Education: Wendell Berry the Professor," in Jason Peters (ed.), *Wendell Berry: Life and Work* (Lexington: University Press of Kentucky, 2007), pp. 137–41.

Hyde, Lewis, *The Gift: How the Creative Spirit Transforms the World* (Edinburgh: Canongate, 2006).

Ingold, Tim, *Lines: A Brief History* (London: Routledge, 2007).

Koestenbaum, Wayne, "'To Be Torn Apart/Is My Ambition': An Interview by Christopher Hennessy," *American Poetry Review* 42, 2 (March 2013): 39–43.

Racter, *The Policeman's Beard Is Half Constructed: Computer Prose and Poetry* (New York: Warner Books, 1984).

Snowdon, David, *Aging with Grace: The Nun Study and the Science of Old Age* (London: Fourth Estate, 2011).

Terrace, H. S., L. A. Petitto, R. J. Sanders and T. G. Bever, "Can an Ape Create a Sentence?," *Science* 206, 4421 (23 November 1979): 891–902.

3. Nouns versus Verbs

Berry, Wendell, "The Pleasures of Eating," in *The World-Eating Fire*, pp. 144–51.

Black, Max, *Models and Metaphors: Studies in Language and Philosophy* (Ithaca: Cornell University Press, 1962).

Bourland, D. David, and Paul Dennithorne Johnston (eds), *To Be or Not: An E-Prime Anthology* (San Francisco: International Society for General Semantics, 1991).

Doty, Mark, *The Art of Description: World into Word* (Minneapolis: Graywolf Press, 2010).

Fenollosa, Ernest, and Ezra Pound, *The Chinese Written Character as a Medium for Poetry: A Critical Edition*, eds. Haun Saussy, Jonathan Stalling and Lucas Klein (New York: Fordham University Press, 2008).

Halliday, M. A. K., "On the Language of Physical Science," in Mohsen Ghadessy (ed.), *Registers of Written English: Situational Factors and Linguistic Features* (London: Pinter, 1988), pp. 162–78.

Hayakawa, S. I., and Alan R. Hayakawa, *Language in Thought and Action*, 5th edn (San Diego: Harcourt Brace Jovanovich, 1990).

Hope, Jonathan, *Shakespeare and Language: Reason, Eloquence and Artifice in the Renaissance* (London: Bloomsbury, 2014).

Lasch, Christopher, *Plain Style: A Guide to Written English* (Philadelphia: University of Pennsylvania Press, 2002).

Merton, Thomas, *Conjectures of a Guilty Bystander* (London: Burns & Oates, 1968).

——, "Is the World a Problem?," in *Thomas Merton: Selected Essays*, ed. Patrick O'Connell (Maryknoll, NY: Orbis Books, 2013), pp. 331–41.

——, *New Seeds of Contemplation* (London: Burns & Oates, 1964).

——, "Rain and the Rhinoceros," in *Raids on the Unspeakable* (New York: New Directions, 1966), pp. 9–26.

——, *The Seven-Storey Mountain* (New York: Harcourt Brace, 1998).

——, "War and the Crisis of Language," in Robert Ginsberg (ed.), *The Critique of War: Contemporary Philosophical Explorations* (Chicago: Henry Regnery, 1969), pp. 99–119.

Sennett, Richard, *Together: The Rituals, Pleasures and Politics of Cooperation* (London: Penguin, 2013).

4. Nothing Like a Windowpane

Adorno, Theodor, "Punctuation Marks," *Antioch Review* 48, 3 (Summer 1990): 300–305.

Auerbach, Erich, *Mimesis: The Representation of Reality in Western Literature*, trans. Willard R. Trask (Princeton: Princeton University Press, 1968).

Barthes, Roland, "African Grammar," in *The Eiffel Tower and Other Mythologies*, trans. Richard Howard (Berkeley: University of California Press, 1997), pp. 103–9.

——, "The Grain of the Voice," in *Image Music Text*, trans. Stephen Heath (London: Fontana, 1977), pp. 179–89.

——, *Roland Barthes*, trans. Richard Howard (London: Macmillan, 1977).

——, *What is Sport?*, trans. Richard Howard (New Haven: Yale University Press, 2007).

Fisher, Marshall, "Memoria Ex Machina," *Harper's* (December 2002).

Gass, William, "The Ontology of the Sentence, or How to Make a World of Words," in *World Within the Word* (New York: Knopf, 1978), pp. 308–38.

Gopnik, Adam, *At the Strangers' Gate* (London: Riverrun, 2017).

Gowers, Ernest, *Plain Words: A Guide to the Use of English* (London: HMSO, 1948).

Kenner, Hugh, "The Politics of the Plain," *New York Times Book Review*, 15 September 1985.

Laubach, Frank, *The Silent Billion Speak* (New York: Friendship Press, 1943).

Lee, Laurie, *Village Christmas: And Other Notes on the Village Year* (London: Penguin, 2016).

McLuhan, Marshall, *Understanding Media: The Extensions of Man* (London: Routledge, 2001).

Paterson, Don, "The Lyric Principle, Part I: The Sense of Sound," *Poetry Review* 97, 2 (Summer 2007): 56–72.

Teems, David, *Tyndale: The Man Who Gave God an English Voice* (London: Thomas Nelson, 2012).

5. The High-wire Act

Barthelme, Donald, "Not-Knowing," in *Not Knowing: The Essays and Interviews of Donald Barthelme*, ed. Kim Herzinger (New York: Random House, 1997), pp. 11–25.

Bowie, Malcolm, *Proust Among the Stars* (London: Fontana, 1998).

Christensen, Francis, *Notes Towards a New Rhetoric: Six Essays for Teachers* (New York: Harper & Row, 1967).

Flesch, Rudolf, "Let's Face the Facts about Writing: A Look at Our Common Problems," *College English* 12, 1 (October 1950): 19–24.

——, "Teaching Bureaucrats Plain English," *College English* 7, 8 (May 1946): 470–74.

——, *The Art of Plain Talk* (New York: Harper & Row, 1946).

Friedwald, Will, *Sinatra! The Song is You: A Singer's Art* (New York: Scribner, 1995).

Gopen, George D., and Judith A. Swan, "The Science of Scientific Writing," *American Scientist* 78, 6 (November–December 1990): 550–58.

Graves, Robert, *Mammon and the Black Goddess* (London: Cassell, 1965).

Gunning, Robert, *The Technique of Clear Writing* (New York: McGraw-Hill, 1968).

Halliday, M. A. K., "Differences Between Spoken and Written Language: Some Implications for Literacy Teaching," in *Language and Education*, ed. Jonathan J. Webster (London: Continuum, 2007), pp. 63–80.

Millier, Brett C., *Elizabeth Bishop: Life and the Memory of It* (Berkeley: University of California Press, 1993).

Petit, Philippe, *On the High Wire*, trans. Paul Auster (New York: Random House, 1985).

Trevelyan, G. M., *An Autobiography and Other Essays* (London: Longman, 1949).

Weathers, Winston, "The Rhetoric of the Series," *College Composition and Communication* 17, 5 (December 1966): 217–22.

6. Foolish Like a Trout

Csikszentmihalyi, Mihaly, *Flow: The Classic Work on How to Achieve Happiness* (London: Rider, 2002).

"David Abbott," in *The Copy Book* (Crans: RotoVision, 1995), pp. 10–13.

Gardner, John, *The Art of Fiction: Notes on Craft for Young Writers* (London: Vintage, 2001).

Gopen, George, *The Sense of Structure: Writing from the Reader's Perspective* (New York: Pearson, 2004).

Gornick, Vivian, *The Situation and the Story: The Art of Personal Narrative* (New York: Farrar, Straus and Giroux, 2002).

Haussamen, Brock, "The Future of the English Sentence," *Visible Language* 28, 1 (Winter 1994): 4–25.

Hugo, Richard, *The Triggering Town: Lectures and Essays on Poetry and Writing* (New York: Norton, 1979).

Kirschenbaum, Matthew, *Track Changes: A Literary History of Word Processing* (Cambridge, MA: Harvard University Press, 2016).

Lee, Hermione, *The Novels of Virginia Woolf* (London: Methuen, 1977).

Lewis, Edwin Herbert, *The History of the English Paragraph* (Chicago: Chicago University Press, 1894).

Lutz, Gary, "The Sentence is a Lonely Place," *The Believer* (January 2009).

Lynch, Kevin, *The Image of the City* (Cambridge, MA: MIT Press, 1960).

McPhee, John, *Draft No. 4: On the Writing Process* (New York: Farrar, Straus and Giroux, 2017).

Monson, Ander, "The Essay as Hack," in Carl H. Klaus and Ned Stuckey-French (eds.), *Essayists on the Essay: Montaigne to Our Time* (Iowa City: University of Iowa Press, 2012), pp. 177–9.

Norman, Donald, *The Design of Everyday Things* (London: MIT Press, 1998).

——, *The Invisible Computer* (Cambridge, MA: MIT Press, 1998).

Pettinger, Peter, *Bill Evans: How My Heart Sings* (New Haven: Yale University Press, 2002).

Pinker, Steven, *The Sense of Style: The Thinking Person's Guide to Writing in the 21st Century* (London: Allen Lane, 2014).

Prose, Francine, *Reading Like a Writer: A Guide for People Who Love Books and for Those Who Want to Write Them* (London: Aurum Press, 2012).

Quack this Way: David Foster Wallace & Bryan A. Garner Talk Language and Writing (Dallas: RosePen Books, 2013).

Rosen, Charles, *Piano Notes: The Hidden World of the Pianist* (London: Allen Lane, 2003).

Tomalin, Nicholas, *Nicholas Tomalin Reporting* (London: André Deutsch, 1975).

Winters, David, "An Interview with Gordon Lish," *Critical Quarterly* 57, 4 (December 2015): 89–104.

7. A Small, Good Thing

Hale, Sheila, *The Man Who Lost His Language* (London: Allen Lane, 2002).

Hall, Donald, *Life Work* (Boston: Beacon Press, 1993).

Judt, Tony, *The Memory Chalet* (London: Vintage, 2011).

Lopez, Barry, *About This Life: Journeys on the Threshold of Memory* (London: Harvill Press, 1999).

Luria, A. R., *The Man with a Shattered World: The History of a Brain Wound*, trans. Lynn Solotaroff (Cambridge, MA: Harvard University Press, 1987).

Mabey, Richard, *Nature Cure* (London: Chatto & Windus, 2005).

Acknowledgments

These, like sentences, should take up no more space than they need. My thanks for help, suggestions and edits to Rebecca Bailey, Jim Barnard, Andrew Croft, Jo Croft, Alice Ferrebe, Cecily Gayford, Elspeth Graham, Lynsey Hanley, Liam Moran, Michael Moran, Wynn Moran, Glenda Norquay, Gerry Smyth, Karolina Sutton and Kate Walchester. Thanks to Caroline Pretty for her scrupulous but sensitive copyediting, and special thanks to my editor Daniel Crewe for all his careful reading and encouragement. And to the students who have made me think about sentences: my thanks and apologies for using you as material, for which I offer in inadequate reparation this single sentence.

My dad, Michael Moran, died suddenly while this book was in press. He was also an academic and writer, and we would read and edit each other's writing via e-mail. I so wanted us to carry on writing sentences together, but instead I have to offer up this book in memory of him, with love and gratitude.

Index